EXERCISES

to Accompany

A CANADIAN

WRITER'S

REFERENCE

DIANA HACKER

UPDATED
SECOND
EDITION

Prince George's Community College

NELSON

✦

™

THOMSON LEARNING

Australia • Canada • Mexico • Singapore • Spain • United Kingdom • United States

NELSON

THOMSON LEARNING™

Exercises to Accompany A Canadian Writer's Reference, Updated Second Edition

by Diana Hacker

Editorial Director and Publisher:
Evelyn Veitch

Acquisitions Editor:
Kelly Torrance

Marketing Manager:
Don Thompson

Production Editor:
Bob Kohlmeier

Production Coordinator:
Hedy Sellers

Proofreader:
Wayne Herrington

Art Director:
Angela Cluer

Cover Design:
Peggy Rhodes

Compositor:
Tammy Gay

Printer:
Webcom

Canadian Cataloguing in Publication Data

Hacker, Diana, date
Exercises to accompany A Canadian writer's reference, Updated 2nd ed.

ISBN 0-17-616925-3

1. English language – Rhetoric – Problems, exercises, etc. 2. English language – Grammar – Problems, exercises, etc. I. Hacker, Diana, date. Canadian writer's reference. II. Title.

PE1408.H33 2000 Suppl.   808'.042
C00-932265-5

A Note for Instructors

The exercise sets in this booklet are keyed to specific sections in *A Canadian Writer's Reference*. If you have adopted *A Canadian Writer's Reference* as a text, you are welcome to photocopy any or all of these exercises for a variety of possible uses:

— as homework
— as classroom practice
— as quizzes
— as individualized self-teaching assignments
— as a support for a writing centre or learning lab

This exercise booklet is also available for student purchase.

The exercises are double-spaced, and the instructions ask students to edit the sentences with cross-outs and insertions, not simply to recopy them with corrections. Students will thus receive practice in the same editing techniques they are expected to apply in their own drafts.

Most exercise sets begin with an example that is done for the student, followed by five lettered sentences for which answers are provided in the back of the booklet. The sets then continue with five or ten numbered sentences whose answers are given in the instructor's answer key only. If you want students to work independently, checking all of their revision themselves, you may of course reproduce the answer key.

A Note for Students

The exercises in this booklet are designed to accompany *A Canadian Writer's Reference*. To benefit from them, you must first read the corresponding section in the book (such as E1, Parallelism), which is illustrated with sentences similar to those in the exercises.

Most of the exercise sets consist of five lettered sentences and five or ten numbered sentences. Answers to the lettered sentences appear in the back of this booklet so that you may test your understanding without the help of an instructor. Instructors use the numbered sentences for a variety of purposes — as homework or as quizzes, for example. If your instructor prefers that you use all of the exercise sentences for self-study, he or she may provide you with an answer key to both the lettered and the numbered sentences.

All exercises are double-spaced, allowing you to edit the sentences with cross-outs and insertions instead of recopying whole sentences. *A Canadian Writer's Reference* shows you how to edit, and a sample sentence at the beginning of each exercise set demonstrates the technique. Editing is the revision technique used by nearly all practising writers. You will find that it has three important advantages over recopying: It is much faster, it allows you to focus on the problem at hand, and it prevents you from introducing new errors as you revise.

Contents

Basic Grammar

Answers to Lettered Exercises

EXERCISE E1-1   Parallelism   If you have problems with this exercise, see pp. 63–65 in
A Canadian Writer's Reference, Updated Second Edition.

Edit the following sentences to correct faulty parallelism. Revisions of lettered sentences appear
in the back of the booklet. Example:

> requesting
> We began the search by calling the Department of Social Services and ~~requested~~ a list
> of licensed day-care centres in our area.

a. The system has capabilities such as communicating with other computers, processing records, and mathematical functions.

b. The personnel officer told me that I would answer the phone, welcome visitors, distribute mail, and some typing.

c. Nolan helped by cutting the grass, trimming shrubs, mulching flowerbeds, and leaf raking.

d. How ideal it seems to raise a family here in Cap de la Madeleine instead of the air-polluted suburbs.

e. Michiko told the judge that she had been pulled out of a line of fast-moving traffic and of her perfect driving record.

1. The summer of our engagement, we saw a few plays, attended family outings, and a few parties.

2. At the arts and crafts table, the children make potholders, key rings, weave baskets, paint, and assemble model cars.

3. The examiners observed us to see if we could stomach the grotesque accidents and how to cope with them.

4. During basic training, I was not only told what to do but also what to think.

5. Activities on Wednesday afternoons include fishing trips, dance lessons, and computers.

6. Bill finds it harder to be fair to himself than being fair to others.

7. More plants fail from improper watering than any other cause.

8. Your adviser familiarizes you with the school and how to select classes appropriate for your curriculum.

9. My job involves teaching, marking papers, and I attend department meetings.

10. The babysitter was expected to feed two children, entertain them, take phone messages, and some cleaning in the kitchen.

EXERCISE E2-1   Needed words   If you have problems with this exercise, see pp. 65–68 in *A Canadian Writer's Reference*, Updated Second Edition.

Add any words needed for grammatical or logical completeness in the following sentences. Revisions of lettered sentences appear in the back of the booklet. Example:

> that
> **The officer at the desk feared ⌃ the prisoner in the interrogation room would escape.**

a.   Myra was both interested and concerned about the contents of her father's will.

b.   A few of the day-care services are similar to the public schools.

c.   SETI (the Search for Extraterrestrial Intelligence) has and will continue to excite interest among space buffs.

d.   Samantha got along better with the chimpanzees than Albert.

e.   We were glad to see Jasper National Park was recovering from the devastating forest fire.

1.   Their starting salaries are higher than other professionals with more seniority.

2.   For many years Canadians had trust and affection for Barbara Frum.

3.   In my opinion, her dependence on tranquilizers is no healthier than the alcoholic or the addict.

4.   When the fishing trip was cancelled, my mother was as disappointed, if not more disappointed than, my father.

5.   Many people do not believe the provincial government should spend money on supporting run-away teenagers.

6.   St. John's is larger than any city in Newfoundland.

7.   Great-Uncle John's car resembled other bootleggers: it had a smoke screen device useful in case of pursuit by the police.

8.   Darryl was both gratified and apprehensive about his scholarship to the University of Toronto.

9.   The driver went to investigate, only to find one of the supposedly new tires had blown.

10.   It was obvious that the students liked the new teacher more than the principal.

EXERCISE E3-1 Misplaced modifiers If you have problems with this exercise, see pp. 68–70 in *A Canadian Writer's Reference*, Updated Second Edition.

Edit the following sentences to correct misplaced or awkwardly placed modifiers. Revisions of lettered sentences appear in the back of the booklet. Example:

in a telephone survey
Answering questions can be annoying. in a telephone survey.

a. He only wanted to buy three roses, not a dozen.

b. Within the next few years, orthodontists will be using the technique Kurtz developed as standard practice.

c. Celia received a flyer about a workshop on making a kimono from a Japanese nun.

d. Jurors are encouraged to carefully and thoroughly sift through the evidence.

e. Each province would set a program into motion of recycling all reusable products.

1. We hope Monica will realize that providing only for her children's material needs is harmful before it is too late.

2. The orderly confessed that he had given a lethal injection to the patient after ten hours of grilling by the police.

3. Several recent studies have encouraged heart patients to more carefully watch their cholesterol levels.

4. Mike, as the next wave rolled in, dropped in easily and made a smooth turn, but the wave closed out.

5. He promised never to remarry at her deathbed.

6. The recordings were all done at the studio of the late Jimi Hendrix named Electric Ladyland.

7. The old Marlboro ads depicted a man on a horse smoking a cigarette.

8. Sid only wanted to see the end of the film again, not the full two hours.

9. The RCMP was falsely accused of mishandling the attempted assassination by the media.

10. The adoption agency informed us that we would be able to at long last get a child.

EXERCISE E3-2   Dangling modifiers   If you have problems with this exercise, see pp. 71–72 in *A Canadian Writer's Reference*, Updated Second Edition.

Edit the following sentences to correct dangling modifiers. Most sentences can be revised in more than one way. Revisions of lettered sentences appear in the back of the booklet. Example:

a student must complete

To acquire a degree in almost any field, two science courses. must be completed.

a.   Reaching the heart, a bypass was performed on the severely blocked arteries.

b.   Nestled in the cockpit, the pounding of the engine was muffled only slightly by my helmet.

c.   While dining at night, the lights along the Baja coastline created a romantic atmosphere perfect for our first anniversary.

d.   While still a beginner at tennis, the coaches recruited my sister to train for the Olympics.

e.   After returning to Jamaica, Marcus Garvey's "Back to Africa" movement slowly died.

1.   When flashing, do not speed through a yellow light.

2.   Exhausted from battling the tide and the undertow, a welcome respite appeared in the swimmer's view—the beach!

3.   While standing in front of the school chatting with friends, Quay approached me shyly and asked me for a date.

4.   As president of the Library Association, one of Grandmother's duties is to raise money for new acquisitions.

5.   When investigating burglaries and thefts, it was easy for me to sympathize with the victims because I had been a victim myself two years ago.

6.   Spending four hours on the operating table, a tumour as large as a golf ball was removed from the patient's stomach.

7.   As a child growing up in Nigeria, my mother taught me to treat all elders with respect.

8.   At the age of twelve, my social studies teacher entered me in a public speaking contest.

9.   Although too expensive for her budget, Arun bought the computer.

10.   While looking at the map, a police officer approached and asked if she could help.

EXERCISE E4-1   Shifts   If you have problems with this exercise, see pp. 72–75 in *A Canadian Writer's Reference*, Updated Second Edition.

Edit the following sentences to eliminate distracting shifts. Revisions of lettered sentences appear in the back of the booklet. Example:

they

For most people quitting smoking is not easy once ~~you~~ are hooked.

a. The young man who burglarized our house was sentenced to probation for one year, a small price to pay for robbing one of their personal possessions as well as of their trust in other human beings.

b. After the count of three, Mikah and I placed the injured woman on the scoop stretcher. Then her vital signs were taken by me.

c. A minister often has a hard time because they have to please so many different people.

d. We drove for eight hours until we reached the Alberta Badlands. You could hardly believe the eeriness of the landscape at dusk.

e. The question is whether ferrets bred in captivity have the instinct to prey on prairie dogs or is this a learned skill.

1. Police officers always follow strict codes of safety. For example, always point the barrel of the gun upward when the gun is not in use.

2. One person collects the tickets and another will search the concert patrons for drugs.

3. One young aide, Kay, was very unprofessional. Curse words were used to quiet the children.

4. The polygraph examiner will ask if you have ever stolen goods on the job, if you have ever taken drugs, and have you ever killed or threatened to kill anyone.

5. A single parent often has only their ingenuity to rely on.

6. When the director travels, you will make the hotel and airline reservations and you will arrange for a rental car. A detailed itinerary must also be prepared.

7. As I was pulling in the decoys, you could see and hear the geese heading back to the bay.

8. Rescue workers put water on her face and lifted her head gently onto a pillow. Finally, she opens her eyes.

9. With self-discipline and a desire to improve oneself, you too can enjoy the benefits of running.

10. We always follow a strict routine at the campground. First we erected the tent, rolled out the sleeping bags, and set up the kitchen; then we all head for the swimming pool.

EXERCISE E5-1   Mixed constructions   If you have problems with this exercise, see pp. 75–77 in *A Canadian Writer's Reference*, Updated Second Edition.

Edit the following sentences to untangle mixed constructions. Revisions of lettered sentences appear in the back of the booklet. Example:

> ~~By~~ Ḻoosening the soil around your jade plant will help the air and nutrients penetrate to the roots.

a. My instant reaction was filled with anger and disappointment.

b. I brought a problem into the house that my mother wasn't sure how to handle it.

c. It is through the misery of others that has made old Harvey rich.

d. A cloverleaf is when traffic on limited-access freeways can change direction.

e. Bowman established the format in which future football card companies would emulate for years to come.

1. The more experienced pilots in the system François assigned two aircraft to them.

2. Depending on the number and strength of drinks, the amount of time that has passed since the last drink, and one's body weight determine the concentration of alcohol in the blood.

3. On the third day, my name and a boy named Stephen were called to go down to the office.

4. By pushing the button for the insert mode opens the computer's memory.

5. The reason the Inuit were forced to eat their dogs was because the caribou, on which they depended for food, migrated out of reach.

6. The shelter George stayed in required the men to leave at nine in the morning, in which they had to take their belongings with them.

7. Mei-Ling had to train herself on a mainframe computer that was designed for data entry but it was not intended for word processing.

8. In this box contains the key to your future.

9. Who would have thought that a department store salesperson could be a life-threatening job?

10. Using surgical gloves is a precaution now worn by dentists to prevent contact with the patients' blood and saliva.

EXERCISE E6-1   Coordination and subordination   If you have problems with this exercise, see pp. 78–81 in *A Canadian Writer's Reference*, Updated Second Edition.

In the following paragraphs, combine choppy sentences by subordinating minor ideas or by coordinating ideas of equal importance. More than one effective revision is possible.

Some scientists favour continued research to advance the technology of genetic engineering. They argue that they are only refining the process of selective breeding that has benefited society for many years. For centuries, they claim, scientists have recognized variations in plant and animal species from generation to generation. In the early nineteenth century, scientists explained those variations as part of an evolutionary process. They called this process natural selection. Later scientists found ways to duplicate this process of natural selection. They did not want to leave the process to chance. They developed the technique of selective breeding.

Dairy farmers use selective breeding. They do it to increase production from their herds. They choose the best milk-producing cows for breeding. These cows have certain genetic traits. These traits make them top producers. Breeding them selectively increases the chance that the offspring will inherit those same genetic traits. Then they will be top producers too. For the same reasons, farmers identify the cows that are low producers. They choose not to use them for breeding.

Scientists argue that genetic engineering is not much different from selective breeding. They claim that it can produce similar positive results. Society, they say, should support their research. Society can only benefit, as it has in the past.

EXERCISE E6-2   Coordination and subordination   If you have problems with this exercise, see pp. 78–81 in *A Canadian Writer's Reference*, Updated Second Edition.

Combine or restructure the following sentences by subordinating minor ideas or by coordinating ideas of equal importance. You must decide which ideas are minor because the sentences are given out of context. Revisions of lettered sentences appear in the back of the booklet. Example:

>   *where*
> **The crew team finally returned to shore, ~~and~~ they had a party on the beach**
>   *to celebrate*
> **~~and celebrated~~ the start of the season.**

a. My grandfather has dramatic mood swings, and he was diagnosed as manic-depressive.

b. The losing team was made up of superstars. These superstars acted as isolated individuals on the court.

c. Chantal had helped François through school, and he decided to do the same for her.

d. The aides help the children with reading and math. These are the children's weakest subjects.

e. My first sky dive was from an altitude of 4200 metres, and it was the most frightening experience of my life.

1. Bay Street is located in the heart of downtown Toronto. It is the financial centre of the city.

2. I noticed that the sky was glowing orange and red. I bent down to crawl into the bunker.

3. Our waitress was costumed in a kimono. She had painted her face white. She had arranged her hair in an upswept lacquered beehive.

4. Cocaine is an addictive drug and it can seriously harm you both physically and mentally, if death doesn't get you first.

5. These particles are known as "stealth liposomes," and they can hide in the body for a long time.

6. At the airport I was met by my host mother, Madame Kimmel. She was a very excitable woman who knew absolutely no English.

7. She walked up to the pitcher's mound. She dug her toe into the ground. She swung her arm around backward and forward. Then she threw the ball and struck the batter out.

8. My cat is overweight, and I put him on a diet.

9. The lift chairs were going around very fast. They were bumping the skiers into their seats.

10. I purchased my John Deere tractor five years ago. It needs a number of parts replaced. They are the brakes, the clutch, and the gears.

EXERCISE E6-3 Faulty subordination   If you have problems with this exercise, see pp. 78–81 in *A Canadian Writer's Reference*, Updated Second Edition.

In each of the following sentences, the idea that the writer wished to emphasize is buried in a subordinate construction. Restructure each sentence so that the independent clause expresses the major idea and lesser ideas are subordinated. Revisions of lettered sentences appear in the back of the booklet. Example:

Though
^Catherine has weathered many hardships, ~~though~~ she has rarely become discouraged.

[Emphasize that Catherine has rarely become discouraged.]

a. We experienced a routine morning at the clinic until an infant in cardiac arrest arrived by an ambulance. *[Emphasize the arrival of the infant.]*

b. My 1969 Camaro, which is no longer street legal, is an original SS396. *[Emphasize the fact that the car is no longer street legal.]*

c. I presented the idea of job sharing to my supervisors, who to my surprise were delighted with the idea. *[Emphasize the supervisors' response to the idea.]*

d. Although some aboriginal groups try to preserve their ancestors' sacred customs, outsiders have forced changes on them. *[Emphasize the aboriginals' attempt to preserve their customs.]*

e. Sophia's country kitchen, which overlooks a field where horses and cattle graze among old tombstones, was formerly a lean-to porch. *[Emphasize that the kitchen overlooks the field.]*

1. My grandfather, who raised his daughters on his own, was born eighty-six years ago in Italy. *[Emphasize how the grandfather raised his daughters.]*

2. I was losing consciousness when my will to live kicked in. *[Emphasize the will to live.]*

3. Louis's team worked with the foreign mission by building new churches and restoring those damaged by hurricanes. *[Emphasize the building and restoring.]*

4. The rotor hit, gouging a hole about three millimetres deep in my helmet. *[Emphasize the fact that the rotor gouged a hole in the helmet.]*

5. Although Sarah felt that we lacked decent transportation, our family owned a Jeep, a pickup truck, and a sports car. *[Emphasize Sarah's feeling that the family lacked decent transportation.]*

EXERCISE E7-1 Sentence variety If you have problems with this exercise, see pp. 82–83 in *A Canadian Writer's Reference*, Updated Second Edition.

Edit the following paragraph to increase variety in sentence structure.

I have spent thirty years of my life on a tobacco farm, and I cannot understand why people smoke. The whole process of raising tobacco involves deadly chemicals. The ground is treated for mould and chemically fertilized before the tobacco seed is ever planted. The seed is planted and begins to grow, and then the bed is treated with weed killer. The plant is then transferred to the field. It is sprayed with poison to kill worms about two months later. Then the time for harvest approaches, and the plant is sprayed once more with a chemical to retard the growth of suckers. The tobacco is harvested and hung in a barn to dry. These barns are havens for birds. The birds defecate all over the leaves. After drying, these leaves are divided by colour, and no feces are removed. They are then sold to the tobacco companies. I do not know what the tobacco companies do after they receive the tobacco. I do not need to know. They cannot remove what I know is in the leaf and on the leaf. I don't want any of it to pass through my mouth.

EXERCISE W1-1   Usage   If you have problems with this exercise, see the Glossary of Usage, pp. 87–100 in *A Canadian Writer's Reference*, Updated Second Edition.

Edit the following sentences for problems in usage. If a sentence is correct, write "correct" after it. Revisions of lettered sentences appear in the back of the booklet. Example:

> _an_
> **The pediatrician gave my daughter a̶ injection for her allergy.**

a. The amount of horses a Blackfoot warrior had in his possession indicated the wealth of his family.

b. The cat just set there watching his prey.

c. We will contact you by phone as soon as the tickets arrive.

d. What is the capital of Brazil?

e. Habib redesigned the boundary plantings to try and improve the garden's overall design.

1. When he learned that I had seven children, four of which were still at home, Gilles smiled and said that he loved children.

2. Will you except the offer?

3. Please phone for an hotel reservation at the Chateau Laurier in Ottawa.

4. Gary decided to loan his cousin money for a year's tuition.

5. These are the kind of problems that can take months to correct.

6. His conscious troubled him because he had lied.

7. I usually shop first at Kensington Market, which is further away, and then stop at Zehrs on my way home.

8. The Japanese bather could care less whether you use your washcloth as a fig leaf.

9. Alan had been lying on the sidewalk unconscious for nearly two hours before help arrived.

10. Laying on the operating table, I could hear only the beating of my heart.

EXERCISE W2-1 Wordy sentences If you have problems with this exercise, see pp. 101–4 in *A Canadian Writer's Reference*, Updated Second Edition.

Edit the following sentences for wordiness. Revisions of lettered sentences appear in the back of the booklet. Example:

> *even though*
> **The Wilsons moved into the house ~~in spite of the fact that~~ the back door was only ten yards from the train tracks.**

a. The drawing room in the west wing is the room that is said to be haunted.

b. Dr. Singh has seen problems like yours countless numbers of times.

c. In my opinion, Bloom's race for the premiership is a futile exercise.

d. If there are any new fares, then they must be reported by message to our transportation offices in Montreal, Ottawa, and Toronto.

e. In the heart of Beijing lies the Forbidden City, which is an imperial palace built in very ancient times during the Ming dynasty.

1. Seeing the barrels, the driver immediately slammed on his brakes.

2. The thing data sets are used for is communicating with other computers.

3. The town of Banff, located in Alberta, was founded as a vacation spot for British travellers.

4. In the early eighties, some analysts viewed Soviet expansion as an effort to achieve nothing less than world dominance, if not outright control of the world.

5. You will be the departmental travel coordinator for all members of the department.

6. Martin Luther King, Jr., was a man who set a high standard for future leaders to meet.

7. Your task will be the deliverance of correspondence to all employees of the company.

8. A typical autocross course consists of at least two straightaways, and the rest of the course is made up of numerous slaloms and several sharp turns.

9. The program is called the Weight Control Program, and it has been remarkably successful in helping airmen and airwomen lose weight.

10. The price of driving while drunk or while intoxicated can be extremely high.

EXERCISE W2-2 Wordy sentences If you have problems with this exercise, see pp. 101–4 in *A Canadian Writer's Reference*, Updated Second Edition.

Edit the following paragraph to eliminate wordiness.

We examined the old house from top to bottom. In fact, we started in the attic, which was hot and dusty, and made our way down two flights of stairs, and down one more descent, which was a spiral staircase, into the basement. On our way back up, we thought we heard the eerie noise, the one that had startled us from our sound sleep in the first place. This time the noise was at the top of the staircase that led to the second-floor hallway. We froze and stood quietly at exactly the same moment, listening very intently. Finally, after a few moments, someone said, "Why don't we all go in together and see what it is?" Cautiously, with great care, we stepped over the threshold into the dark hallway, which disappeared into darkness in front of us. There was an unearthly emanating light shining from underneath the door that led into the kitchen. All at once we jumped when we heard a loud crashing sound from behind that door. Before we could rush into the kitchen at high speed, the light went out suddenly, and instantly we were in total pitch black darkness. I thought I heard someone's teeth chattering; then I realized with a shock that it was my own teeth I heard chattering. Without saying a word, we backed silently away from the kitchen door—no one wanted to go in now. Then it was as if someone had shot off a gun, because before we realized what we were doing, we tore up the stairs as fast as we could, and we dove into our beds and pulled the covers up and over us to shut out any more frightening sounds and thoughts.

EXERCISE W3-1   Jargon and pretentious language   If you have problems with this exercise, see pp. 104–5 in *A Canadian Writer's Reference*, Updated Second Edition.

Edit the following sentences to eliminate jargon, pretentious or flowery language, and euphemisms. You may need to make substantial changes in some sentences. Revisions of lettered sentences appear in the back of the booklet. Example:

>   learned   office
> **After two weeks in the legal department, Jana has ~~worked into~~ the routine,**
>   performance has
> **~~of the office~~ and her ~~functional and self-management skills have~~ exceeded all**
> **expectations.**

a. It is a widespread but unproven hypothesis that the parameters of significant personal change for persons in midlife are extremely narrow.

b. Have you ever been accused of flagellating a deceased equine?

c. In 1985 I purchased a residential property that was in need of substantial upgrading.

d. When Sal was selected out from his high-paying factory job, he learned what it was like to be economically depressed.

e. Passengers should endeavour to finalize the customs declaration form prior to exiting the aircraft.

1. In my youth, my family was under the constraints of difficult material circumstances.

2. As I approached the edifice of confinement where my brother was incarcerated, several inmates loudly vocalized a number of lewd remarks.

3. The nurse announced that there had been a negative patient-care outcome due to a therapeutic misadventure on the part of the surgeon.

4. When we returned from our evening perambulation, we shrank back in horror as we surmised that our domestic dwelling was being swallowed up in hellish flames.

5. The bottom line is that the company is experiencing a negative cash flow.

Name _____ Section _____ Date _____

EXERCISE W3-2 Slang and level of formality If you have problems with this exercise, see pp. 106–7 in *A Canadian Writer's Reference*, Updated Second Edition.

Edit the following paragraph to eliminate slang and maintain a consistent level of formality.

The graduation speaker really blew it. He should have discussed the options and challenges facing the graduating class. Instead, he shot his mouth off at us and trashed us for being lazy and pampered. He did make some good points, however. Our profs have certainly babied us by not holding fast to deadlines, by dismissing assignments that the class ragged them about, by ignoring our tardiness, and by handing out easy C's like hotcakes. Still, we resented this speech as the final word from the university establishment. It should have been the orientation speech when we started university.

EXERCISE W3-3 Sexist language If you have problems with this exercise, see pp. 108–9 in *A Canadian Writer's Reference*, Updated Second Edition.

Edit the following sentences to eliminate sexist language or sexist assumptions. Revisions of lettered sentences appear in the back of the booklet. Example:

> Scholarship athletes
> ~~A scholarship athlete~~ must be as concerned about ~~his~~ their academic performance as
> they are   their
> ~~he is~~ about ~~his~~ athletic performance.

a. Mrs. Asha Purpura, who is a doctor's wife, is the defence attorney appointed by the court. Al Jones has been assigned to work with her on this case.

b. If a young graduate is careful about investments, he can accumulate a significant sum in a relatively short period.

c. An elementary school teacher should understand the concept of nurturing if she intends to be a success.

d. Because Dr. Brown and Dr. Dorothy Coombs were the senior professors in the department, they served as co-chairmen of the promotion committee.

e. If man does not stop polluting his environment, mankind will perish.

1. I have been trained to doubt an automobile mechanic, even if he has an excellent reputation.

2. After a new prime minister is elected, he must assemble his cabinet.

3. In the recent provincial election, Lena Weiss, a defence lawyer and mother of two, easily defeated Harvey Tower, an architect.

4. In my home town, the lady mayor has led the fight for a fair share of federal funds for new schools.

5. As partners in a successful real estate firm, John Crockett and Sarah Cooke have been an effective sales team: He is particularly skilful at arranging attractive mortgage packages; she is a vivacious blonde who is especially successful at telemarketing.

EXERCISE W4-1 Active verbs If you have problems with this exercise, see pp. 111–12 in *A Canadian Writer's Reference*, Updated Second Edition.

Revise any weak, unemphatic sentences by replacing *be* verbs or passive verbs with active alternatives. Some sentences are emphatic; do not change them. Revisions of lettered sentences appear in the back of the booklet. Example:

> The park ranger doused the campfire before giving us
> ~~The campfire was doused by the park ranger before we were given~~ a ticket for
>
> **unauthorized use of a campsite.**

a. Her letter was in acknowledgment of the students' participation in the literacy program.

b. The entire operation is managed by Ahmed, the producer.

c. Finally the chute caught air and popped open with a jolt at about 700 metres.

d. There were fighting players on both sides of the rink.

e. At the crack of thunder, my cat jumped from the windowsill and landed on my dog below, who was crawling under the sofa.

1. Just as the police closed in, two shots were fired by the terrorists from the roof of the hotel.

2. Julia was successful in her first attempt to pass the bar exam.

3. The starting gates flew open and the horses thundered onto the track.

4. C.B.'s are used to find parts, equipment, food, lodging, and anything else that is needed by a trucker.

5. Yellow flags were thrown down by all the referees.

EXERCISE W4-2   Misused words   If you have problems with this exercise, see pp. 112–13 in *A Canadian Writer's Reference*, Updated Second Edition.

Edit the following sentences to correct misused words. Revisions of lettered sentences appear in the back of the booklet. Example:

> all-absorbing
> **The training required for a ballet dancer is** ~~all absorbent~~.

a. Many of us are not persistence enough to make a change for the better.

b. It is sometimes difficult to hear in church because the agnostics are so terrible.

c. Tyrone has a presumptive attitude.

d. When bp nichol died at age forty, he left a legacy of poems that will make him immortal for years to come.

e. This patient is kept in isolation to prevent her from obtaining our germs.

1. Waste, misuse of government money, security and health violations, and even pilfering have become major dilemmas at the FBI.

2. Trifle, a popular English dessert, contains a ménage of ingredients that do not always appeal to Canadian tastes.

3. The University of British Columbia, which is situated in Point Grey, is surrounded on three sides by water.

4. Frequently I cannot do my work because the music blaring from my son's room detracts me.

5. Tom Jones is an illegal child who grows up under the care of Squire Western.

EXERCISE W4-3   Standard idioms   If you have problems with this exercise, see pp. 113–14 in *A Canadian Writer's Reference*, Updated Second Edition.

Edit the following sentences to eliminate errors in the use of idiomatic expressions. If a sentence is correct, write "correct" after it. Answers to lettered sentences appear in the back of the booklet. Example:

> by
> **We agreed to abide ~~with~~ the decision of the judge.**
>   ^

a.   Queen Anne was so angry at Sarah Churchill that she refused to see her again.

b.   Prior to the Russians' launching of *Sputnik, nik* was not an English suffix.

c.   Try and come up with the rough outline, and Marika will fill in the details.

d.   For the frightened refugees, the dangerous trek across the mountains was preferable than life in a war zone.

e.   The parade moved off of the street and onto the beach.

1.   Be sure and report on the danger of releasing genetically engineered bacteria into the atmosphere.

2.   Why do you assume that embezzling bank assets is so different than robbing the bank?

3.   Most of the class agreed to Cuong's view that nuclear proliferation is potentially a very dangerous problem.

4.   What type of a wedding are you planning?

5.   Andrea intends on joining the CUSO after graduation.

EXERCISE W4-4 Clichés and mixed figures of speech   If you have problems with this exercise, see pp. 114–15 in *A Canadian Writer's Reference*, Updated Second Edition.

Edit the following sentences to replace worn-out expressions and clarify mixed figures of speech. Revisions of lettered sentences appear in the back of the booklet. Example:

> the colour drained from his face.
> **When he heard about the accident, he turned white as a sheet.**
>   ^

a. Pierrette told Kyle that keeping skeletons in the closet would be playing with fire.

b. The prime minister thought that the scientists were using science as a sledgehammer to grind their political axes.

c. Ours was a long courtship; we waited ten years before finally deciding to tie the knot.

d. We ironed out the sticky spots in our relationship.

e. Sasha told us that he wasn't willing to put his neck out on a limb.

1. I could read him like a book; he had egg all over his face.

2. Tears were strolling down the child's face.

3. High school is a seething caldron of raw human emotion.

4. There are too many cooks in the broth here at corporate headquarters.

5. Once she had sunk her teeth into it, Helen burned through the assignment.

EXERCISE G1-1   Subject–verb agreement   If you have problems with this exercise, see pp. 121–27 in *A Canadian Writer's Reference*, Updated Second Edition.

Underline the subject (or compound subject) of the sentence or clause and then select the verb that agrees with it. (If you have difficulty identifying the subject, consult B2-a.) Answers to lettered sentences appear in the back of the booklet. Example:

> **<u>Someone</u> in the audience (has/have) volunteered to participate in the experiment.**

a. Your friendship over the years and your support on a wide variety of national issues (has/have) meant a great deal to us.

b. Two-week-old onion rings in the ashtray (is/are) not a pretty sight.

c. Each of the twenty-five actors (was/were) given a five-minute tryout, and only three of us were called back for a more intensive audition.

d. The main source of income for Trinidad (is/are) oil and pitch.

e. When I returned to the town where I was born, I found there (was/were) no signs of the old baseball field or remnants of the bleachers.

1. The chances of your being awarded a scholarship (is/are) high.

2. Quilts made by the Amish (commands/command) high prices.

3. Located at the south end of the complex (was/were) an Olympic-size pool, two basketball courts, and four tennis courts.

4. The most significant lifesaving device in automobiles (is/are) seat belts.

5. The old iron gate and the brick wall (makes/make) our courthouse appear older than its fifty years.

6. The dangers of smoking (is/are) well documented.

7. There (was/were) a Peanuts cartoon and a few Mother Goose rhymes pinned to the bulletin board.

8. When food supplies (was/were) scarce, we had to arrange to have some flown in.

9. The slaughter of pandas for their much-sought-after pelts (has/have) caused the panda population to decline dramatically.

10. Hidden under the floorboards (was/were) a bag of coins and a rusty sword.

EXERCISE G1-2   Subject–verb agreement   If you have problems with this exercise, see pp. 121–27 in *A Canadian Writer's Reference*, Updated Second Edition.

Edit the following sentences for problems with subject–verb agreement. If a sentence is correct, write "correct" after it. Answers to lettered sentences appear in the back of the booklet. Example:

were
Jack's first days on the job <s>was</s> gruelling.

a. High concentrations of carbon monoxide results in headaches, dizziness, unconsciousness, and even death.

b. Not until my interview with Dr. Hwang were other possibilities opened to me.

c. After hearing the evidence and the closing arguments, the jury was sequestered.

d. Crystal chandeliers, polished floors, and a new oil painting has transformed Sandra's apartment.

e. Either Gertrude or Alice take the dog out for its nightly walk.

1. Small pieces of fermented bread was placed around the edge of the platter.

2. Of particular concern are penicillin and tetracycline, antibiotics used to make animals more resistant to disease.

3. The presence of certain bacteria in our bodies is one of the factors that determine our overall health.

4. Nearly everyone on the panel favour the temporary moratorium on cod fishing in Newfoundland.

5. Every year a number of kokanee salmon, not native to the region, is introduced into Flathead Lake.

6. Measles is a contagious childhood disease.

7. Neither Paul nor Arthur is usually here on Sundays.

8. At MGM Studios at Disney World, the wonders of movie making comes alive.

9. She is the only one of our professors who emphasize the role of the student in learning.

10. The key program of Alcoholics Anonymous are the twelve steps to recovery.

EXERCISE G1-3   Subject–verb agreement   If you have problems with this exercise, see pp. 121–27 in *A Canadian Writer's Reference*, Updated Second Edition.

In the following paragraphs, circle the verb in parentheses that agrees with its subject.

Natalie, together with many other students in her educational philosophy class, (supports/support) a program to standardize cultural literacy in the high-school curriculum. Natalie and those who agree with her (argues/argue) that students should have a broad background of shared knowledge. This shared knowledge (helps/help) bind a culture together and (encourages/encourage) pride in our country's heritage. In deciding which knowledge to include in a standardized curriculum, advocates of cultural literacy (looks/look) primarily to the past: If a book (has/have) stood the test of time, they say, it is a part of our culture worth preserving.

Kimberly and several other students in the class (opposes/oppose) the idea of a standardized high-school curriculum. They argue that the content of such a curriculum is not easily determined in a multicultural society, especially in subjects such as sociology, history, and literature that (examines/examine) values and beliefs. Kimberly and other opponents of cultural literacy (believes/believe) that knowledge survives over time because a dominant culture preserves it. Kimberly (doesn't/don't) question the value of that knowledge, but she recognizes that the dominant culture over the years (neglects/neglect) to preserve and transmit knowledge that is important to less powerful cultures. The important factor in this debate (is/are) the students: Each of them (deserves/deserve) attention and respect. Kimberly worries that plans to standardize cultural literacy (ignores/ignore) the cultures of too many students. She represents those in her class who (feels/feel) that a true cultural literacy program has to include knowledge from many cultures and that standardizing a multi-cultural curriculum may not be practical on any large scale.

EXERCISE G2-1 Irregular verbs If you have problems with this exercise, see pp. 127–31 in *A Canadian Writer's Reference*, Updated Second Edition.

Edit the following sentences for problems with irregular verbs. If a sentence is correct, write "correct" after it. Answers to lettered sentences appear in the back of the booklet. Example:

>   *saw*
> **Was it you I ~~seen~~ last night at the concert?**
>   ^

a. Noticing that my roommate was shivering and looking pale, I rung for the nurse.

b. When I get the urge to exercise, I lay down until it passes.

c. Grandmother had drove our new jeep to the cottage on Georgian Bay, so we were left with the station wagon.

d. I just heard on the news that Michael Smith has broke the world record for the long jump.

e. For thousands of years, people have lain under the stars and gazed into the night sky.

1. How many times have you swore to yourself, "I'll diet tomorrow, after one more piece of cheesecake"?

2. Laying there in a bed of wet leaves with mist falling lightly on my face, I could hear Linda call my name, but I never answered, not even to say I was alive.

3. The burglar must have gone immediately upstairs, grabbed what looked good, and took off.

4. In just a week the ground had froze, and the first winter storm had left over a foot of snow.

5. All parents were asked to send a mat for their children to lay on.

6. Lincoln took good care of his legal clients; the contracts he drew for the Illinois Central Railroad could never be broke.

7. Have you ever dreamed that you were falling from a cliff or flying through the air?

8. I locked my brakes, leaned the motorcycle to the left, and laid it down to keep from slamming into the fence.

9. In her third year, Celine run the 10-K in 33:16.

10. Larry claimed that he had drank a bad pop, but Esther suspected the truth.

EXERCISE G2-2   *-s* and *-ed* **verb forms and omitted verbs**   If you have problems with this exercise, see pp. 132–35 in *A Canadian Writer's Reference*, Updated Second Edition.

Edit the following sentences for problems with *-s* and *-ed* verb forms and for omitted verbs. If a sentence is correct, write "correct" after it. Answers to lettered sentences appear in the back of the booklet. Example:

>   has   doesn't
> **The psychologist ~~have~~ so many problems in her own life that she ~~don't~~ know how to advise anyone else.**

a. I love to watch Pierre as he leaps off the balance beam and lands lightly on his feet.

b. The museum visitors were not suppose to touch the exhibits.

c. Our church has all the latest technology, even a close-circuit television.

d. We often don't know whether he angry or just joking.

e. Staggered working hours have reduce traffic jams and save motorists many litres of gas.

1. The bald eagle feed mostly on carrion, such as the carcasses of deer or the bodies of dead salmon.

2. Have there ever been a time in your life when you were too depressed to get out of bed?

3. We were ask to sign a contract committing ourselves to not smoking for forty-eight hours.

4. Today a modern school building covers most of the old grounds.

5. Christos didn't know about Stephen's death because he never listens. He always talking.

6. The training for security checkpoint screeners, which takes place in an empty airplane hangar, consist of watching out-of-date videos.

7. Our four children plays one or two instruments each.

8. The ball was pass from one player to the other so fast that even the TV crew miss some of the exchanges.

9. Do he have enough energy to hold down two jobs while going to night school?

10. How would you feel if a love one had been a victim of a crime like this?

EXERCISE G2-3   Verb tense and mood   If you have problems with this exercise, see pp. 135–40 in *A Canadian Writer's Reference*, Updated Second Edition.

Edit the following sentences to eliminate errors in verb tense or mood. If a sentence is correct, write "correct" after it. Answers to lettered sentences appear in the back of the booklet. Example:

> had been
> **After the path ~~was~~ ploughed, we were able to walk through the park.**
> ^

a.   The palace of Knossos in Crete is believed to have been destroyed by fire around 1375 B.C.E.

b.   Watson and Crick discovered the mechanism that controlled inheritance in all life: the workings of the DNA molecule.

c.   In 1941 Hitler decided to kill the Jews. But Himmler and his SS were three years ahead of him; they had mass murder in mind since 1938.

d.   Toni could be an excellent student if she wasn't so distracted by problems at home.

e.   Ken recommended that Michel remain on the beginners' slope for at least a week.

1.   Our neighbour stood at the door looking so pale and ashen that we thought he just saw a ghost.

2.   They had planned to have adopted a girl, but they got twin boys.

3.   My sister Deanna was outside playing with the new puppies that were born only a few weeks earlier.

4.   As soon as my aunt applied for the position of pastor, the post was filled by an inexperienced seminary graduate who had been so hastily snatched that his mortarboard was still in midair.

5.   Sheila knew that Bruce would have preferred to have double-dated, but she really wanted to be alone with him.

6.   Don Quixote, in Cervantes' novel, was an idealist ill suited for life in the real world.

7.   The tornado tore up the palm trees, lifted them over the hotel roof, and had dropped them onto the car.

8.   I would like to have been on the *Mayflower* but not to have lived through that first winter.

9.   When the doctor said "It's a girl," I was thrilled. All my life I dreamed about having a daughter.

10.   If men and women were angels, no government would be necessary.

EXERCISE G2-4 Active and passive voice If you have problems with this exercise, see p. 141 in *A Canadian Writer's Reference*, Updated Second Edition.

In the following paragraphs, the italicized passive verbs are less effective than active verbs would be. Replace each italicized passive verb with an active verb. Be prepared to discuss why the remaining verbs (printed in brackets) are appropriate.

Although Professor Whist works as a consultant for several corporations that manufacture electrical generating equipment, he [is known and respected] by environmentalists as an advocate for the preservation of natural resources. Professor Whist feels that his influence *can be used* to affect corporate decisions concerning the environment. The environment *is protected* to some extent by many corporations, but when someone with Professor Whist's reputation *is hired* by them, their public image *is improved* too.

Although Professor Whist [is besieged] by many groups for his expertise, he continues to teach. For part of every class a discussion *is led* about how the environment *is affected* by everyday decisions of big corporations as well as of ordinary people. Each semester, for example, students learn that electricity [is produced] by a very inefficient process, with only about 35 percent of the potential energy in coal, oil, or uranium converting directly into electricity. Students also learn that simple steps *can be taken* at home to conserve every type of energy that *is used*. Professor Whist believes that he can make a difference, and his conviction *is demonstrated* by his personal example in the conference room and in the classroom.

EXERCISE G3-1   Pronoun–antecedent agreement   If you have problems with this exercise, see pp. 142–45 in *A Canadian Writer's Reference*, Updated Second Edition.

Edit the following sentences to eliminate problems with pronoun-antecedent agreement. Most of the sentences can be revised in more than one way, so experiment before choosing a solution. If a sentence is correct, write "correct" after it. Revisions of lettered sentences appear in the back of the booklet. Example:

> Recruiters
> ~~The recruiter~~ may tell the truth, but there is much that they choose not to tell.

a. I can be standing in front of a photocopier, with parts scattered around my feet, and someone will ask me to let them make a copy.

b. The undergraduate students elect their executive board tomorrow.

c. The instructor has asked everyone to bring their own tools to carpentry class.

d. An eighteenth-century architect was also a classical scholar; they were often at the forefront of archeological research.

e. On the first day of class, Mr. Bhatti asked each individual why they wanted to stop smoking.

1. If a driver refuses to take a blood or breath test, he or she will have their licences suspended for six months.

2. Why should we care about the timber wolf? One answer is that they have proven beneficial to humans by killing off weakened prey.

3. No one should be forced to sacrifice their prized possession—life—for someone else.

4. Seven qualified women applied for the job, each one hoping for a career move that would let them use their skills and education on more than secretarial work.

5. If anyone notices any suspicious activity, they should report it to the police.

6. The crowd grew until they filled not only the plaza but also the surrounding streets.

7. David lent his motorcycle to someone who allowed their friend to use it.

8. By the final curtain, ninety percent of the audience had voted with their feet.

9. A good teacher is patient with his or her students, and they should maintain an even temper.

10. A graduate student needs to be willing to take on a sizable debt unless they have wealthy families.

EXERCISE G3-2 Pronoun–antecedent agreement   If you have problems with this exercise, see pp. 142–45 in *A Canadian Writer's Reference*, Updated Second Edition.

Edit the following paragraphs for problems with pronoun–antecedent agreement. Choose an effective revision strategy that avoids sexist language.

John found himself surrounded by students who were returning to college after an absence of more than fifteen years, and they shared his nervousness. No one knew what changes they should expect. Because Alice and Rakesh had been in the same situation last year, Dean Shell asked each of them to share their experiences during an orientation workshop. Neither John nor the other older students allowed his schedule to interfere with the workshop.

Rakesh mentioned that the biggest surprise for him had been the extensive use of computers. Fifteen years ago, he recalled, a math student rarely did their homework on a computer. Now, he said, no one has to do their assignments without the help of a software program. Rakesh asked the audience if it remembered erasable bond paper and correction tape, and they groaned, recalling the frustration of typing term papers. Now, said Rakesh, a student can write their papers in the campus computer labs.

Alice said that a returning student would also be surprised when they saw how the course content had changed. Every department, she said, had found their own way of incorporating the work of women and minorities in their courses. And almost all the departments had pooled their resources to create interdisciplinary courses. A student shouldn't be surprised, Alice said, to find a novel assigned in their sociology class or an oral history project featured in their English class. A final surprise, Alice noted, is the extent to which writing is now emphasized across the curriculum—in the sciences, the social sciences, and even math.

After hearing Rakesh and Alice share their positive experience, the audience felt that many of its fears were unfounded, and they looked forward to the coming semesters.

EXERCISE G3-3   Pronoun reference   If you have problems with this exercise, see pp. 145–47 in *A Canadian Writer's Reference*, Updated Second Edition.

Edit the following sentences to correct errors in pronoun reference. In some cases you will need to decide on an antecedent that the pronoun might logically refer to. Revisions of lettered sentences appear in the back of the booklet. Example:

> **Many other companies besides Bell Canada now offer long-distance phone service.**
> The competition
> ~~This~~ has led to lower long-distance rates.
> ^

a. The detective removed the bloodstained shawl from the body and then photographed it.

b. In Professor Jamal's class, you are lucky to earn a C.

c. Please be patient with the elderly residents that have difficulty moving through the cafeteria line.

d. The settlers' lifestyle was particularly difficult; they had to clear acres of trees and cope with an extreme climate.

e. All students can secure parking permits from the campus police office; they are open from 8 A.M. until 8 P.M.

1. He recognized her as the woman which had won an Olympic gold medal for swimming.

2. Many people believe that the polygraph test is highly reliable if you employ a licensed examiner.

3. We expect the concert to last for at least two hours. Since the average ticket sells for twenty dollars, this was not being unrealistic.

4. In Ogden Nash's verse, he always manages to give me a laugh about every other line.

5. Since the tutors are so helpful, it gives us the opportunity to learn more.

6. When Uncle Jim put the cake on the table, it collapsed.

7. Employees are beginning to take advantage of the company's athletic facilities. They offer squash and tennis courts, a small track, and several trampolines.

8. Be sure to visit Istanbul's bazaar, where they sell everything from Persian rugs to electronic calculators.

9. If you have a sweet tooth, you can visit the confectioner's shop, where it is still made as it was a hundred years ago.

10. Time and time again, I fell for materialistic guys that gave me nothing but pain.

EXERCISE G3-4   Pronoun case: personal pronouns   If you have problems with this exercise, see pp. 147–50 in *A Canadian Writer's Reference*, Updated Second Edition.

Edit the following sentences to eliminate errors in case. If a sentence is correct, write "correct" after it. Answers to lettered sentences appear in the back of the booklet. Example:

> **Grandfather cuts down trees for neighbours much younger than ~~him~~. he.**

a.   My Ethiopian neighbour was puzzled by the dedication of we joggers.

b.   The jury was astonished when the witness suddenly confessed that the murderer was none other than he.

c.   Sue's husband is ten years older than her.

d.   Everyone laughed whenever Sandra described how her brother and her had seen the Loch Ness monster and fed it sandwiches.

e.   There is only a slim chance of his getting an infection from the procedure.

1.   Doctors should take more seriously what us patients say about our treatment.

2.   Grandfather said he would give anything to live nearer to Paulette and me.

3.   The patient began suffering from the delusion that him and his family were constantly being followed and observed.

4.   A professional counsellor advised the division chief that Marco, Ella, and myself should be allowed to apply for the opening.

5.   Because of last night's fire, we are fed up with him drinking and smoking.

6.   The student ethics board gave Maxine and I the opportunity to defend ourselves against the instructor's false charges.

7.   The swirling cyclone caused he and his horse to race for shelter.

8.   The officer found my mother and me standing on the basement steps peering down at the "prowlers," a family of raccoons.

9.   During the testimony the witness pointed directly at the defendant and announced that the thief was her.

10.   Despite our different backgrounds, a close friendship developed between Susumu and I.

EXERCISE G3-5   Pronoun case: *who* **and** *whom*   If you have problems with this exercise, see pp. 151–52 in *A Canadian Writer's Reference*, Updated Second Edition.

Edit the following sentences to eliminate errors in the use of *who* and *whom* (or *whoever* and *whomever*). If a sentence is correct, write "correct" after it. Answers to lettered sentences appear in the back of the booklet. Example:

> whom
> What is the name of the person ~~who~~ you are sponsoring for membership in the club?
>   ^

a. In his first production of *Hamlet*, who did Laurence Olivier replace?

b. Who was Martin Luther King's mentor?

c. Datacall allows you to talk to whoever needs you, no matter where you are in the building.

d. Some group leaders cannot handle the pressure; they give whomever makes the most noise most of their attention.

e. One of the women who Lanvis hired became the most successful lawyer in the agency.

1. When medicine is scarce and expensive, physicians must give it to whomever has the best chance to survive.

2. Who was accused of receiving Mafia funds?

3. They will become business partners with whomever is willing to contribute to the company's coffers.

4. The only highway travellers who get flat tires are the ones whom do not carry a spare.

5. The elderly woman who I was asked to take care of was a clever, delightful companion.

EXERCISE G3-6 Pronoun case If you have problems with this exercise, see pp. 147–52 in *A Canadian Writer's Reference*, Updated Second Edition.

Edit the following paragraph to correct errors in pronoun case. (See G3-c and G3-d.)

After our first year, my friend Kim and me were trying to decide if we wanted to major in business administration. Dr. Bane, an economics professor who we had first semester, agreed to talk with Kim and I. At first, Kim did not seem as interested in a business career as I, but then Dr. Bane explained to us neophytes how many options are open to business graduates. Neither Kim nor myself had realized that the possibilities are so interesting. Dr. Bane told us about a recent graduate whom she felt was one of her most promising students: He owns and manages his own bookstore. Another recent graduate, who Dr. Bane almost flunked senior year, is a buyer for a chain of clothing stores. Dr. Bane was surprised at her becoming successful so soon, but she said there's a niche for everyone in business. Dr. Bane cautioned us with a story about another graduate who was interested only in whomever would pay her the most. "Money isn't everything," Dr. Bane said. "Your being well matched to your work is more important than earning large sums of money." She then invited us, both Kim and I, to her fourth-year seminar in which students discuss their internships. When we thanked Dr. Bane for his advice, she told Kim and me that it probably would not be hard for we too to find our niche in business.

EXERCISE G4-1 Adjectives and adverbs If you have problems with this exercise, see pp. 152–56 in *A Canadian Writer's Reference*, Updated Second Edition.

Edit the following sentences to eliminate errors in the use of adjectives and adverbs. If a sentence is correct, write "correct" after it. Answers to lettered sentences appear in the back of the booklet. Example:

> **When I watched Carl run the 5-K on Saturday, I was amazed at how ~~good~~ he paced himself.**
>
> *well*

a. When Tina began breathing normal, we could relax.

b. All of us on the team felt badly about our performance.

c. Tim's friends cheered and clapped very loud when he made it to the bottom of the beginners' slope.

d. The vaulting box, commonly known as the horse, is the easiest of the four pieces of equipment to master.

e. Last Christmas was the most perfect day of my life.

1. When answering the phone, you should speak clearly and courteous.

2. Doug wanted to know which of the two airlines offered the cheapest fares.

3. We wanted a hunting dog. We didn't care if he smelled badly, but we really did not want him to smell bad.

4. In the early 1970s, chances for survival of the bald eagle looked real slim.

5. After checking to see how bad I had been hurt, my sister dialed 911.

6. Mr. Miller visits his doctor regularly for a complete physical.

7. Professor Brown's public praise of my performance on the exam made me feel a little strangely.

8. Of all my relatives, Uncle Max is the most cleverest.

9. The hall closet is so filled with ski equipment that the door won't hardly close.

10. The green bagels looked and tasted real peculiar.

EXERCISE G5-1 Sentence fragments If you have problems with this exercise, see pp. 156–61 in *A Canadian Writer's Reference*, Updated Second Edition.

Repair any fragment by attaching it to a nearby sentence or by rewriting it as a complete sentence. If a word group is correct, write "correct" after it. Revisions of lettered sentences appear in the back of the booklet. Example:

> **One Greek island that should not be missed is Mykonos/, A vacation spot for Europeans and a playpen for the rich.**

a. As I stood in front of the microwave, I recalled my grandmother bending over her old black stove. And remembered what she taught me: that any food can have soul if you love the people you are cooking for.

b. It has been said that there are only three indigenous American art forms. Jazz, musical comedy, and soap opera.

c. I stepped on some frozen moss and started sliding down the face of a flat rock toward the falls. Suddenly I landed on another rock.

d. We need to stop believing myths about drinking. That strong black coffee will sober you up, for example, or that a cold shower will straighten you out.

e. As we walked up the path, we came upon the gun batteries. Large grey concrete structures covered with ivy and weeds.

1. Sitting at a sidewalk café near the Sorbonne, I could pass as a French student. As long as I kept my mouth shut.

2. Mother loved to play all our favourite games. Canasta, Monopoly, hide-and-seek, and even kick the can.

3. The horses were dressed up with hats and flowers. Some even wore sunglasses.

4. I had pushed these fears into one of those quiet places in my mind. Hoping they would stay there asleep.

5. To give my family a comfortable, secure home life. That is my most important goal.

6. If a woman from the desert tribe showed anger toward her husband, she was whipped in front of the whole village. And shunned by the rest of the women.

7. A tornado is a violent whirling wind. One that produces a funnel-shaped cloud and moves over land in a slim path of destruction.

8. The pleasure gardens of eighteenth-century European cities offered a variety of diversions. Such as dancing, gambling, dining, and promenading.

9. In my three years of driving, I have never had an accident. Not one wreck, not one fender-bender, not even a little dent.

10. The pilots ejected from the burning plane, landing in the water not far from the ship. And immediately popped their flares and life vests.

EXERCISE G5-2   Sentence fragments   If you have problems with this exercise, see pp. 156–61 in *A Canadian Writer's Reference,* Updated Second Edition.

Repair each fragment in the following paragraphs by attaching it to a sentence nearby or by rewriting it as a complete sentence.

Until recently, Pauline thought that studying a second language would not be very useful. Because she was going to be a business major, training for management. Even if she worked for a company with an office overseas, she was sure that international clients would communicate in English. The accepted language of the world marketplace. But Pauline's adviser, Professor Will, told her that many Canadian firms are owned by foreign corporations. Or rely on the sales of subsidiaries in foreign markets. English is therefore not always the language of preference.

Professor Will advised Pauline to learn a second language. Such as French, German, or Japanese. These are the most useful languages, he told her. In addition to preparing her to use the language, the classes would expose her to the history, culture, and politics of another country. Factors that often affect business decisions. After talking with Professor Will, Pauline was convinced. To begin immediately to prepare for her business career by studying a second language.

EXERCISE G6-1   Comma splices and fused sentences   If you have problems with this
exercise, see pp. 161–66 in *A Canadian Writer's Reference*, Updated Second Edition.

Revise any comma splices or fused sentences using the method of revision suggested in brackets.
Revisions of lettered sentences appear in the back of the booklet. Example:

> Because
> ‸Abdul was obsessed with his weight, he rarely ate anything sweet and delicious.
>
> *[Restructure the sentence.]*

a. The city had one public swimming pool, it stayed packed with children all summer long.
    [Restructure the sentence.]

b. The building is being renovated, therefore at times we have no heat, water, or electricity. *[Use
    a comma and a coordinating conjunction.]*

c. Why should we pay taxes to support public transportation, we prefer to save energy dollars
    by carpooling. *[Make two sentences.]*

d. We all make mistakes no one is perfect. *[Use a semicolon.]*

e. In Garvey's time the caste system in the West Indies was simple, the lighter the skin tone, the
    higher the status. *[Use a colon.]*

1. For the first time in her adult life, Lucia had time to waste, she could spend a whole day
    curled up with a good book. *[Use a semicolon.]*

2. Be sure to take your credit card, Disney has a way of making you want to spend money.
    [Restructure the sentence.]

3. The next time an event is cancelled because of bad weather, don't blame the meteorologist,
    blame nature. *[Make two sentences.]*

4. While we were walking down Queen Street, Gary told us about his Aunt Elsinia, she was an
    extraordinary woman. *[Restructure the sentence.]*

5. The president of Algeria was standing next to the podium he was waiting to be introduced.
    [Restructure the sentence.]

6. On most days I had only enough money for bus fare, lunch was a luxury I could not afford.
    [Use a semicolon.]

7. There was one major reason for Jean-Pierre's wealth, his grandfather had been a multimillion-
    aire. *[Use a colon.]*

8. John positioned himself next to the smartest girl in class, he wouldn't cheat, of course, but it was comforting to know that the right answer was not far away. *[Make two sentences.]*

9. Of the many geysers in Yellowstone National Park, the most famous is Old Faithful, it sometimes reaches 50 metres in height. *[Restructure the sentence.]*

10. Before we arrived at the retirement home, I had learned a lot about Great-Uncle Bjorn, he had been a regular man-about-town in his day. *[Restructure the sentence.]*

EXERCISE G6-2 Comma splices and fused sentences If you have problems with this exercise, see pp. 161–66 in *A Canadian Writer's Reference*, Updated Second Edition.

Revise any comma splices or fused sentences using a technique that you find effective. If a sentence is correct, write "correct" after it. Revisions of lettered sentences appear in the back of the booklet. Example:

but

I ran the three blocks as fast as I could, ~~however~~ I still missed the bus.

a. The trail up Mount Grossmore was declared impassable, therefore, we decided to return to our hotel a day early.

b. The duck hunter set out his decoys in the shallow bay and then settled in to wait for the first real bird to alight.

c. The instructor never talked to the class, she just assigned make-work and sat at her desk reading the newspaper.

d. Researchers were studying the fertility of Canada geese they X-rayed all the female geese to see how many eggs they had.

e. The suburbs seemed cold, they lacked the warmth and excitement of our Italian neighbourhood.

1. Are you able to endure boredom, isolation, and potential violence, then the army may well be the adventure for you.

2. Jet funny cars are powered by jet engines, these engines are the same type that are used on fighter aircraft and helicopters.

3. If one of the dogs should happen to fall through the ice, it would be cut loose from the team and left to its fate, the sled drivers could not endanger the rest of the team for just one dog.

4. The volunteers worked hard to clean up and restore calm after the tornado, as a matter of fact, many of them did not sleep for the first three days of the emergency.

5. Nuclear power plants produce energy by fission, a process that generates radioactive waste.

6. After days of struggling with her dilemma, Rosa came to a decision, she would sacrifice herself for her people and her cause.

7. The College of Arts is made up of eight departments, each has its own chair.

8. We didn't trust her, she had lied before.

9. I pushed open the first door with my back, turning to open the second door, I encountered a young woman in a wheelchair holding it open for me.

10. If you want to lose weight and keep it off, consider this advice, don't try to take it off faster than you put it on.

EXERCISE G6-3   Comma splices, fused sentences, and fragments   If you have problems with this exercise, see pp. 161–66 in *A Canadian Writer's Reference*, Updated Second Edition.

In the following rough draft, repair any sentence fragments and revise any comma splices or fused sentences.

Teri, Karen, and I took introductory foreign language courses last year. Each of us was interested in learning a different language, however, we were all trying to accomplish the same goal. To begin mastering a new language. When we compared our classes and the results, we found that each course used a quite different approach to language learning.

In my Spanish course, Professor Cruz introduced lists of new vocabulary words every week, she devoted half of each class to grammar rules. I spent most of my time memorizing lists and rules. In addition to vocabulary and grammar study, I read passages of Spanish literature. Translating them into English. And wrote responses to the reading in Spanish. The only time I spoke Spanish, however, was when I translated a passage or answered questions in class. Although Professor Cruz spoke Spanish for the entire class period.

Instead of memorizing vocabulary lists and grammar rules and translating reading selections, Teri's Portuguese class rehearsed simple dialogues useful for tourists. Conducting every class in Portuguese, Teri's professor asked students to recite the dialogues, she corrected the students' pronunciation and grammar as they spoke. Teri's homework was to go to the language lab, she listened to various dialogues and practised ordering meals, asking for directions to a train station, and so on. Teri learned to pronounce the language well, she mastered the simple dialogues. But she did not get much practice in reading.

Karen took a course in Russian, her experience was different from Teri's and from mine. Her professor asked the students to read articles from the Russian press. And to listen to recent news programs from Russia. In class, students discussed the articles and programs. Karen's professor encouraged the students to use Russian as much as possible in their discussions, she also allowed them to use English. Other class activities included writing letters in response to articles in Russian publications and role playing to duplicate real-life situations. Such as a discussion with a neighbour about the lack of meat in the shops. Karen learned to understand spoken Russian and to speak the language, in addition, she regularly practised reading and writing. Although her Russian course was difficult, Karen thinks it will help her when she visits Russia this summer.

Of the three of us, Karen is the most positive about her course. She is certain that she will further develop her language skills when visiting Russia, moreover, she is confident that she can communicate without struggling too much with a dictionary. Teri and I feel less positive about our courses. Because we both have forgotten the vocabulary and grammar rules. If I were asked to read a passage in Spanish now, I couldn't, Teri says she would not understand Portuguese or be able to respond to a single dialogue if she had to.

EXERCISE T1-1 Articles If you have problems with this exercise, see pp. 169–72 in *A Canadian Writer's Reference*, Updated Second Edition.

Articles have been omitted from the following story, adapted from *Zen Flesh, Zen Bones*, compiled by Paul Reps. Insert the articles *a*, *an*, and *the* where English requires them and be prepared to explain the reasons for your choices.

Moon Cannot Be Stolen

Ryokan, who was Zen master, lived simple life in little hut at foot of mountain. One evening thief visited hut only to discover there was nothing in it to steal.

Ryokan returned and caught him. "You may have come long way to visit me," he told prowler, "and you should not return empty-handed. Please take my clothes as gift." Thief was bewildered. He took Ryokan's clothes and slunk away. Ryokan sat naked, watching moon. "Poor fellow," he mused, "I wish I could give him this beautiful moon."

EXERCISE T1-2 Articles If you have problems with this exercise, see pp. 169–72 in *A Canadian Writer's Reference*, Updated Second Edition.

Edit the following sentences for problems with articles. Suggested revisions of lettered sentences appear in the back of the booklet. Example:

> The
> Money I was carrying in my wallet was not enough to pay for a train ticket.

a. Some of the best wine in world comes from Rhine River valley in southwestern Germany.

b. A courage is admirable characteristic.

c. When I was at the park yesterday I saw dog playing with ball. I picked up ball and threw it, and dog chased after it.

d. She got advice from her counsellor, but advice was not as helpful as she had hoped.

e. The beauty is a difficult concept to define.

1. She poured glass of milk and gave glass to her daughter.

2. The broccoli is extremely nutritious vegetable.

3. She refused to eat the broccoli on her plate.

4. Even a strongest team in our league would have trouble defeating the Argonauts.

5. Unfortunately, an information is not always easy to find.

EXERCISE T2-1 Helping verbs and main verbs If you have problems with this exercise, see pp. 173–76 in *A Canadian Writer's Reference*, Updated Second Edition.

Revise any sentences in which helping and main verbs do not match. You may need to look at the list of irregular verbs in G2-a to determine the correct form of some irregular verbs. Answers to lettered sentences appear in the back of the booklet. Example:

> **Maureen should finds an apartment closer to campus.**

a. We will making this a better country.

b. There is nothing in the world that TV has not touch on.

c. Did you understood my question?

d. A hard wind was blown while we were climbing the mountain.

e. The child's innocent world has been taking away from him.

1. Children are expose at an early age to certain aspects of adult life.

2. We've spend too much money this month, especially on things we don't really need.

3. Have you find your wallet yet?

4. I have ate Thai food only once before.

5. It would have help to know the cost before the work began.

EXERCISE T2-2   Helping verbs and main verbs   If you have problems with this exercise, see pp. 173–76 in *A Canadian Writer's Reference*, Updated Second Edition.

Revise the following paragraph so that all helping verbs and main verbs match. The paragraph may also include verbs that cannot be used in the progressive sense (such as *know*) or intransitive verbs (such as *occur*), which cannot be used in the passive voice. Example:

               done
He had not yet ~~did~~ the required homework.

As children, Ned and I used to fish from the railroad bridge overlooking the bay. Sometimes we could saw the fish swimming near the surface. In those days, I was believing that we would remained friends forever. I could not have imagining that just a few years later we would rarely speak to each other. But that is what was happened to us. As a teenager, Ned started spending time with people whom I did not like at all. He was drinking too much, and one time he was arresting by the police; they said he had not renew his driver's licence. The last time I saw Ned, he was stood on that same railroad bridge, gazing across the water. I was wanting to say something to him, but I did not know what. I pretended that I have not see him and kept walking.

EXERCISE T2-3 Verbs in conditional sentences   If you have problems with this exercise, see pp. 176–78 in *A Canadian Writer's Reference*, Updated Second Edition.

Edit the following conditional sentences for problems with verbs. In some cases, more than one revision is possible. Suggested revisions of lettered sentences appear in the back of the booklet. Example:

> had
> If I ~~have~~ the money, I would meet my friends in Barcelona next summer.

a. He would have won the election if he went to the northern regions to campaign.

b. If Martin Luther King, Jr., was alive today, he would be appalled by the violence in the inner cities of the United States.

c. Whenever my uncle comes to visit, he brought me an expensive present.

d. We will lose our largest client unless we would update our computer system.

e. If Verena wins a fellowship, she would go to graduate school.

1. If it would not be raining, we could go fishing.

2. If Lee had followed the doctor's orders, he had recovered from his operation by now.

3. You would have met my cousin if you came to the party last night.

4. Whenever I washed my car, it rains.

5. Our son would have drowned if Officer Arsenault didn't risk her life to save him.

EXERCISE T2-4   Verbs in conditional sentences   If you have problems with this exercise, see pp. 176–78 in *A Canadian Writer's Reference*, Updated Second Edition.

For each sentence, fill in the blank with the correct conditional form of the verb in parentheses. In some cases you may not have to change the base form of the verb at all. In many cases it will be necessary to add at least one helping verb. Answers to lettered sentences appear in the back of the booklet. Example:

> would have
> **If I had known he was coming, I ___cleaned___ the house.**
> **(clean)**

a. If she _____ a seat belt, she probably would not have been hurt.
   (wear)

b. When I need money right away, I _____ to a cash machine.
   (go)

c. Unless the price of wheat suddenly drops, farmers _____ a lot of money this year.
   (earn)

d. If my mother _____ here, she would probably complain about the noise.
   (be)

e. If everyone stopped driving cars, the quality of the air we breathe _____ .
   (improve)

1. Whenever I feel like I'm catching a cold, I _____ a lot of orange juice.
   (drink)

2. If they _____ home earlier, they would not have missed their plane.
   (left)

3. If the tests _____ negative, she will be released from the hospital tomorrow.
   (be)

4. Perhaps he _____ better if he had waited a year or two before starting university.
   (do)

5. If I lived within walking distance of my job, I _____ my car.
   (sell)

EXERCISE T2-5 Verbs followed by gerunds or infinitives If you have problems with this exercise, see pp. 178–80 in *A Canadian Writer's Reference*, Updated Second Edition.

_____

Form sentences by adding gerund or infinitive constructions to the following sentence openings. In some cases, more than one kind of construction may be possible. Possible sentences for lettered items appear in the back of the booklet. Example:

> **Please remind** your sister to call me.

a. I enjoy

b. Will you help Samantha

c. The team hopes

d. Jules and his brothers miss

e. The babysitter let

1. Pollen makes

2. The club president asked

3. Next summer we plan

4. Waverly intends

5. Please stop

EXERCISE T2-6   Verbs followed by gerunds or infinitives   If you have problems with this exercise, see pp. 178–80 in *A Canadian Writer's Reference*, Updated Second Edition.

In each sentence, choose either the gerund or the infinitive form of the verbs in parentheses. Answers to lettered sentences appear in the back of the booklet. Example:

> **She plans __to have__ lunch with a friend this afternoon.**
> **(have)**

a. He put off _____ a doctor and tried to avoid _____ about his illness.
(see)   (think)

b. By refusing _____ her taxes, she risked _____ to jail.
(pay)   (go)

c. We encouraged them _____ back to us, but we did not expect them _____ so quickly.
(write)   (reply)

d. They could not imagine _____ without electricity or _____ to work without a car.
(live)   (get)

e. He claimed _____ innocent and denied _____ anything at all about the crime.
(be)   (know)

1. Her lawyer offered _____ the dispute privately, but he decided _____ the matter to
(settle)   (take)
court.

2. We appreciated _____ all those gifts but postponed _____ thank-you notes until we
(receive)   (send)
had more time.

3. She wanted _____ to him, but he pretended not _____ her and looked the other way.
(talk)   (see)

4. He admitted _____ his essay from a book and promised _____ a letter of apology
(copy)   (send)
to the professor.

5. She recalled _____ him once, but she did not remember ever _____ to him again.
(meet)   (speak)

EXERCISE T3-1 Omissions and repetitions   If you have problems with this exercise, see pp. 182–84 in *A Canadian Writer's Reference*, Updated Second Edition.

In the following sentences, add needed subjects or expletives and delete any repeated subjects, objects, or adverbs. Answers to lettered sentences appear in the back of the booklet. Example:

> **Nancy is the woman whom I talked to ~~her~~ last week.**

a. The roses they brought home they cost three dollars each.

b. Are two grocery stores on Elm Street.

c. The prime minister she is the most popular leader in my country.

d. Pavel hasn't heard from the cousin he wrote to her last month.

e. The king, who had served since the age of sixteen, he was an old man when he died.

1. Henri and Nicole they are good friends.

2. Is important to study the grammar of English.

3. The neighbour we trusted he was a thief.

4. I don't use the subway because am afraid.

5. Archeologists have excavated the city where the old Persian kings are buried there.

EXERCISE T3-2   Order of cumulative adjectives   If you have problems with this exercise, see pp. 185–86 in *A Canadian Writer's Reference*, Updated Second Edition.

Using the chart on page 186, arrange the following modifiers and nouns in their proper order. Answers to lettered items appear in the back of the booklet. Example:

> two new French racing bicycles
> **new, French, two, bicycles, racing**

a.   woman, young, an, Vietnamese, attractive

b.   dedicated, a, priest, Catholic

c.   old, her, sweater, blue, wool

d.   delicious, Joe's, Scandinavian, bread

e.   many, cages, bird, antique, beautiful

1.   round, two, marble, tables, large

2.   several, yellow, tulips, tiny

3.   a, sports, classic, car

4.   courtyard, a, square, small, brick

5.   charming, restaurants, Italian, several

EXERCISE T3-3 Order and placement of adjectives and adverbs If you have problems with this exercise, see pp. 185–87 in *A Canadian Writer's Reference*, Updated Second Edition.

Revise the following sentences so that all adjectives and adverbs are in the proper place and order. (You may want to refer to the chart on page 186 of the text.) If a sentence is correct, write "correct" after it. Answers to lettered sentences appear in the back of the booklet. Example:

> an attractive new
> **My brother just bought a new attractive sports car.**

a. We have two grey large cats; one of them has a small patch of white fur around his right eye.

b. The two men, who were young defence lawyers, wore dark long robes.

c. Most mornings he ate reluctantly his breakfast, and sometimes he refused to eat anything at all.

d. She was wearing new blue jeans with a brown wool sweater and a pair of tan leather cowboy boots.

e. When I was a child, my friends and I built a wooden tree house in an old enormous oak tree.

1. A white attractive church spire is a typical sight in many small Maritime towns and villages.

2. When he woke up the next morning, he climbed slowly from his bed, walked into the bathroom, and then studied nervously his face in the big oval mirror.

3. As the big bus left the parking lot, it expelled an enormous cloud of ugly black exhaust.

4. She lived in a brick tall apartment building with ugly cement balconies on each floor.

5. My grandmother has a mahogany beautiful old table in her dining room.

EXERCISE T3-4   Present versus past participles   If you have problems with this exercise, see pp. 187–88 in *A Canadian Writer's Reference*, Updated Second Edition.

Edit the following sentences for proper use of present and past participles. If a sentence is correct, write "correct" after it. Answers to lettered sentences appear in the back of the booklet. Example:

> *excited*
> **Danielle and Monica were very ~~exciting~~ to be going to the Pantages Theatre for the**
> **first time.**

a. Having to listen to everyone's complaints was irritated.

b. The noise in the hall was distracted to me.

c. He was not pleased with his marks last semester.

d. The violence in recent movies is often disgusted.

e. I have never seen anyone as surprised as Mona when she walked through the door and we turned on the lights.

1. Megan worked on her art project for eight hours but still she was not satisfying.

2. That blackout was the most frightened experience I've ever had.

3. I couldn't concentrate on my homework because I was distracted.

4. Three weeks after her promotion, she decided that being the boss was bored.

5. The exhibit on the Alberta Badlands was fascinated.

EXERCISE T3-5   Present versus past participles   If you have problems with this exercise, see pp. 187–88 in *A Canadian Writer's Reference*, Updated Second Edition.

Circle the correct participial form in each sentence. Answers to lettered sentences appear in the back of the booklet. Example:

The book was so (depressed/depressing) that he stopped reading it after the second chapter.

a. In college, I was never very (interested/interesting) in history or the social sciences.

b. The music that her brother listened to was very (annoyed/annoying).

c. Although he could have done better, he felt (satisfied/satisfying) with his score on the exam.

d. She looked (exhausted/exhausting) by the end of the race.

e. His piano teacher's praise was (encouraged/encouraging).

1. I had a (frightened/frightening) dream last night.

2. The game was (excited/exciting) to watch.

3. After he read the directions he felt very (confused/confusing).

4. It was a (disturbed/disturbing) book; she thought about it a lot after she finished it.

5. My father looked (tired/tiring) after his long day at work.

EXERCISE T3-6 Prepositions showing time and place If you have problems with this exercise, see pp. 188–89 in *A Canadian Writer's Reference*, Updated Second Edition.

In the following sentences, replace any prepositions that are not used correctly. If a sentence is correct, write "correct" after it. Answers to lettered sentences appear in the back of the booklet. Example:

$$\overset{\textit{at}}{\text{The play begins } \cancel{\text{on}} \text{ 7:00 P.M.}}$$

a. We spent seven days on June in the beach, and it rained every day.

b. In the 1980s, the gap between the rich and the poor in Canada became wider.

c. Usually she met with her patients on the afternoon, but in that day she stayed at home to take care of her son.

d. The clock is hanging on the wall on the dining room.

e. In Germany it is difficult for foreigners to become citizens even if they've lived at the country for a long time.

1. He sat on his bed in his room at the hotel.

2. Only the adults in the family were allowed to sit on the dining room table; the children ate in another room.

3. If the train is on time, it will arrive on six o'clock at the morning.

4. She licked the stamp, stuck it in the envelope, put the envelope on her pocket, and walked to the nearest mailbox.

5. The mailbox was in the intersection of Avenue Road and Bloor Street.

EXERCISE T3-7 Prepositions showing time and place If you have problems with this exercise, see pp. 188–89 in *A Canadian Writer's Reference*, Updated Second Edition.

In the following sentences, fill in the blanks with either *at*, *on*, or *in*. Answers to the lettered sentences appear in the back of the booklet. Example:

I told Pasquale to meet me ___at___ the bar ___in___ the hotel ___at___ 10 o'clock.

a. _____ Sunday mornings she and her husband sit _____ the kitchen table reading the newspaper.

b. Her plane is scheduled to arrive _____ 9 o'clock _____ the morning _____ November 18.

c. The cat was hiding _____ the grass, gazing _____ two birds _____ a tree.

d. He had to stand _____ a stool to reach the books _____ the highest shelf.

e. She arrived for her 9 o'clock appointment _____ 8:30; her client was expected back _____ about twenty minutes.

1. All morning they sat _____ the table, discussing how they could make their products more popular _____ other countries.

2. The tree stands _____ the back of their yard _____ the edge of their neighbours' property.

3. The house, which they purchased _____ April of 1991, is _____ a quiet street _____ a nice neighbourhood.

4. Because he has to get up so early _____ the morning, he is usually _____ bed by 10 o'clock _____ night.

5. _____ the football field one of the players was holding the ball _____ both hands, waiting for a signal from the referee.

EXERCISE P1-1   The comma: independent clauses, introductory elements   If you have problems with this exercise, see pp. 193–94 in *A Canadian Writer's Reference*, Updated Second Edition.

Add or delete commas where necessary in the following sentences. If a sentence is correct, write "correct" after it. Answers to lettered sentences appear in the back of the booklet. Example:

> **Because it rained all Labour Day, our picnic was rather soggy.**

a. As she was writing up the report, Constable Blanchard heard a strange noise coming from the trash dumpster.

b. The man at the next table complained loudly and the waiter stomped off in disgust.

c. Instead of eating half a cake or two dozen cookies I now grab a banana or an orange.

d. Nursing is physically, and mentally demanding, yet the pay is low.

e. Uncle Sven's dulcimers disappeared as soon as he put them up for sale but he always kept one for himself.

1. When the runaway race car hit the gas tank exploded.

2. He pushed the car beyond the intersection and poured a bucket of water on the smoking hood.

3. Lighting the area like a second moon the helicopter circled the scene.

4. While one of the robbers tied Laureen to a chair, and gagged her with an apron, the other emptied the contents of the safe into a backpack.

5. Many musicians of Bach's time played several instruments, but few mastered them as early or played with as much expression as Bach.

EXERCISE P1-2   The comma: series, coordinate adjectives   If you have problems with this exercise, see pp. 195–96 in *A Canadian Writer's Reference*, Updated Second Edition.

Add or delete commas where necessary in the following sentences. If a sentence is correct, write "correct" after it. Answers to lettered sentences appear in the back of the booklet. Example:

> **We gathered our essentials, took off for the great outdoors, and ignored the fact that**
> **^**
> **it was Friday the 13th.**

a. She wore a black silk cape, a rhinestone collar, satin gloves and high-tops.

b. There is no need to prune, weed, fertilize or repot your air fern.

c. City Café is noted for its spicy vegetarian dishes and its friendly efficient service.

d. Trevor walked through the room with casual elegant grace.

e. My cat's pupils had constricted to small black shining dots.

1. My brother and I found a dead garter snake, picked it up and placed it on Mr. Brown's doorstep.

2. For breakfast the children ordered corn flakes, English muffins with peanut butter and root beers.

3. Patients with severe irreversible brain damage should not be put on life support machines.

4. Cyril was clad in a luminous orange rain suit and a brilliant white helmet.

5. Anne Frank and thousands like her were forced to hide in attics, cellars and secret rooms in an effort to save their lives.

EXERCISE P1-3   The comma: nonrestrictive elements   If you have problems with this exercise, see pp. 196–99 in *A Canadian Writer's Reference*, Updated Second Edition.

Add or delete commas where necessary in the following sentences. If a sentence is correct, write "correct" after it. Answers to lettered sentences appear in the back of the booklet. Example:

> **My youngest sister, who plays left wing on the team, now lives at The Sands, a beach house near Vancouver.**

a.   B. B. King and Lucille, his customized black Gibson have electrified audiences all over the world.

b.   My backpack which is designed to last a lifetime is wearing out.

c.   The woman running for the council seat in Ward Five had a long history of community service.

d.   Shakespeare's tragedy, *King Lear*, was given a splendid performance by the actor, Laurence Olivier.

e.   Douglass's first autobiography, *Narrative of the Life of Frederick Douglass, An American Slave*, was published in 1845.

1.   I had the pleasure of talking to a woman who had just returned from India where she had lived for ten years.

2.   The Irish students knew by heart the exploits of Cuchulain a legendary Irish warrior but they knew nothing about Freud or Marx or any religion but their own.

3.   The gentleman waiting for a prescription is Mr. Rhee.

4.   *Where the Wild Things Are*, the 1964 Caldecott Medal winner, is my nephew's favourite book.

5.   Going on an archeological dig which has always been an ambition of mine seems out of the question this year.

EXERCISE P1-4   Major uses of the comma   If you have problems with this exercise, see pp. 193–200 in *A Canadian Writer's Reference*, Updated Second Edition.

This exercise covers the major uses of the comma described in P1-a, b, c, d, and e. Add or delete commas where necessary. If a sentence is correct, write "correct" after it. Answers to lettered sentences appear in the back of the booklet. Example:

> **Although we invited him to the party, Gerald decided to spend another late night in**
> **^**
> **the computer room.**

a. The whisky stills which were run mostly by farmers and fishermen were about twenty miles from the nearest town.

b. At the sound of a starting pistol the horses surged forward toward the first obstacle, a sharp incline one metre high.

c. Each morning the seventy-year-old woman cleans the barn, shovels manure and spreads clean hay around the milking stalls.

d. The students of Highpoint are required to wear dull green, polyester pleated skirts.

e. Beauty is in the eye of the beholder but glamour is for anyone who can afford it.

1. After the passage of the Civil Rights Act of 1964 the Ku Klux Klan went underground for a few years but the group's racist views did not change.

2. Madeleine's costume was completed with bright red, snakeskin sandals.

3. As the summer slowly passed and we came to terms with Mike's death we visited the grave site less frequently.

4. The lawyer explained the contract, but we weren't sure we understood all of its implications.

5. While vacationing with a relative Theresa was accidentally mistaken for her sister.

6. I called my pup Pitou meaning "puppy" in French, simply because no other name came to mind.

7. Aunt Emilia was an impossible demanding guest.

8. The French Mirage, the fastest airplane in the Colombian air force, was an astonishing machine to fly.

9. There I was with a shiny, red wagon something that no kid could resist.

10. Siddhartha decided to leave his worldly possessions behind and live in the forest by a beautiful river.

EXERCISE P1-5 All uses of the comma If you have problems with this exercise, see
pp. 193–203 in *A Canadian Writer's Reference*, Updated Second Edition.

Add or delete commas where necessary in the following sentences. If a sentence is correct, write
"correct" after it. Answers to lettered sentences appear in the back of the booklet. Example:

> **"Yes, Virginia, there is a Santa Claus," said the editor.**
> ⌃

a. April 13, 1995 is the final deadline for all applications.

b. The coach having bawled us out thoroughly, we left the locker room with his last harsh words
   ringing in our ears.

c. Good technique does not guarantee however, that the power you develop will be sufficient for
   Kyok Pa competition.

d. We all piled into Sadiq's car which we affectionately referred to as the Blue Goose.

e. Please make the check payable to David Kerr D.D.S., not David Kerr M.D.

1. Mr. Mundy was born on July 22, 1939 in Saskatchewan, where his family had lived for four
   generations.

2. It has been reported that the journalist who suggested Eisenhower as a presidential candi-
   date meant Milton not Ike.

3. One substitute for CFC's has environmentalists concerned because it contains chlorine
   which is also damaging to the ozone layer.

4. We pulled into the first apartment complex we saw, and slowly patrolled the parking lots.

5. Eating raw limpets, I found out, is like trying to eat art gum erasers.

6. Cobbled streets too narrow for two cars to pass, were lined with tiny houses leaning so close
   together they almost touched.

7. We wondered how our overweight grandfather could have been the slim groom in the picture,
   but we kept our wonderings to ourselves.

8. "The last flight" she said with a sigh "went out five minutes before I arrived at the airport."

9. The Rio Grande, the border between Texas and Mexico lay before us. It was a sluggish mud-
   filled meandering stream that gave off an odour akin to sewage.

10. Toronto, Ontario is the home of several fine colleges and universities.

EXERCISE P2-1 Unnecessary commas If you have problems with this exercise, see pp. 203–7 in *A Canadian Writer's Reference*, Updated Second Edition.

Delete commas where necessary in the following sentences. If a sentence is correct, write "correct" after it. Answers to lettered sentences appear in the back of the booklet. Example:

Anne Murray has paved the way for artists such as/k.d. lang and Holly Cole.

a. We'd rather spend our money on blue-chip stocks, than speculate on pork bellies.

b. Being prepared for the worst, is one way to escape disappointment.

c. When he heard the groans, he opened the door, and ran out.

d. My father said, that he would move to Nova Scotia, if I would agree to transfer to Dalhousie.

e. I quickly accepted the fact that I was, literally, in third-class quarters.

1. As a child growing up in Jamaica, I often daydreamed about life in Canada.

2. He wore a thick, black, wool coat over his plaid shirt.

3. Often public figures, (Stompin' Tom Connors is a good example) go to great lengths to guard their private lives.

4. She loved early spring flowers such as, crocuses, daffodils, forsythia, and irises.

5. On Pam's wrist, was a tattoo of a dragon chasing a tiger.

6. Douglas Fir, the tallest of the softwoods, grows on the west coast.

7. Charlie believed every word of the story, and expected the Great Pumpkin to rise out of the pumpkin patch at midnight.

8. The kitchen was covered with black soot, that had been deposited by the wood-burning stove, which stood in the middle of the room.

9. Captain Edward Spurlock observed, that the vast majority of crimes in our city are committed by repeat offenders.

10. Many abusive parents were themselves abused children, so they have no history of benevolent experiences, and lack appropriate healthy role models after which to pattern their behaviour as parents.

EXERCISE P3-1 The semicolon and the comma If you have problems with this exercise, see pp. 193–210 in *A Canadian Writer's Reference*, Updated Second Edition.

Add commas or semicolons where needed in the following well-known quotations. If a sentence is correct, write "correct" after it. Answers to lettered sentences appear in the back of the booklet. Example:

If an animal does something, we call it instinct; if we do the same thing, we call it intelligence.
— *Will Cuppy*

a. While there's snow on the roof it doesn't mean the fire has gone out in the furnace.
— *John G. Diefenbaker*

b. No amount of experimentation can ever prove me right a single experiment can prove me wrong.
— *Albert Einstein*

c. Don't talk about yourself it will be done when you leave.   — *Wilson Mizner*

d. The only sensible ends of literature are first the pleasurable toil of writing second the gratification of one's family and friends and lastly the solid cash.   — *Nathaniel Hawthorne*

e. When men talk about defence they always claim to be protecting women and children but they never ask the women and children what they think.   — *Pat Schroeder*

1. Everyone is a genius at least once a year a real genius has his [or her] original ideas closer together.
— *G. C. Lichtenberg*

2. When choosing between two evils I always like to try the one I've never tried before.
— *Mae West*

3. Once the children were in the house the air became more vivid and more heated every object in the house grew more alive.
— *Mary Gordon*

4. America is a country that doesn't know where it is going but is determined to set a speed record getting there.
— *Lawrence J. Peter*

5. I've been rich and I've been poor rich is better.   — *Sophie Tucker*

EXERCISE P3-2   The semicolon and the comma   If you have problems with this exercise, see pp. 193–210 in *A Canadian Writer's Reference*, Updated Second Edition.

Edit the following sentences to correct errors in the use of the comma and the semicolon. If a sentence is correct, write "correct" after it. Answers to lettered sentences appear in the back of the booklet. Example:

> **Love is blind; envy has its eyes wide open.**
>   ^

a. Many people believe that ferrets are vicious little rodents, in fact, ferrets are affectionate animals that tend to bite only out of fear.

b. Canada has been called a country with no identity; although the Canadian devotion to defining their identity is legendary.

c. The first requirement is honesty, everything else follows.

d. I am not fond of opera, I must admit; however, that I was greatly moved by *Les Misérables*.

e. Deaf-REACH runs a group home, which prepares residents to live independently; a daytime activity centre, where walk-in clients receive job training; and a community service centre, which provides counselling and legal representation.

1. When Chao Neng joined the police force in 1991; he had no idea how hard it would be to bury a fellow officer.

2. Martin Luther King, Jr. had not intended to be a preacher, initially, he had planned to become a lawyer.

3. Severe, unremitting pain is a ravaging force; especially when the patient tries to hide it from others.

4. I entered this class feeling jittery and incapable, I leave feeling poised and confident.

5. Some educators believe that Native history should be taught in separate courses, others prefer to see it integrated into survey courses.

EXERCISE P4-1 The colon, the semicolon, and the comma If you have problems with this exercise, see pp. 193–211 in *A Canadian Writer's Reference*, Updated Second Edition.

Edit the following sentences to correct errors in the use of the comma, the semicolon, or the colon. If a sentence is correct, write "correct" after it. Answers to lettered sentences appear in the back of the booklet. Example:

> **Smiling confidently, the young man stated his major goal in life: to be the minister of agriculture before he was thirty.**

a. The second and most memorable week of outdoor camp consisted of five stages: orientation; long treks; rock climbing; white-water rafting; and return to civilization.

b. Among the cancelled classes were: calculus, physics, advanced biology, and English 101.

c. There are only three seasons here: winter, July, and August.

d. For example: Stephen Leacock once said that "the essence of humour is human kindliness."

e. In his introduction to Katharine White's book on gardening, E. B. White describes her writing process: "The editor in her fought the writer every inch of the way; the struggle was felt all through the house. She would write eight or ten words, then draw her gun and shoot them down."

1. The patient survived for one reason, the medics got to her in time.

2. While travelling through France, Fiona visited: the Loire Valley, Chartres, the Louvre, and the McDonald's stand at the foot of the Eiffel Tower.

3. Minds are like parachutes, they function only when open.

4. Historian Robert Kee looks to the past for the source of the political troubles in Ireland: "If blame is to be apportioned for today's situation in Northern Ireland, it should be laid not at the door of men today but of history."

5. Robin sorts the crabs into three groups: males, females, and crabs about to moult.

EXERCISE P5-1   The apostrophe   If you have problems with this exercise, see pp. 212–14 in *A Canadian Writer's Reference*, Updated Second Edition.

Edit the following sentences to correct errors in the use of the apostrophe. If a sentence is correct, write "correct" after it. Answers to lettered sentences appear in the back of the booklet. Example:

> **Marietta lived above the only bar in town, Smiling ~~Jacks.~~** Jack's.

a.   In a democracy anyones vote counts as much as mine.

b.   He received two A's, three B's, and a C.

c.   The puppy's favourite activity was chasing it's tail.

d.   After we bought J.J. the latest style pants and shirts, he decided that last years faded, ragged jeans were perfect for all occasions.

e.   A crocodiles' life span is about thirteen years.

1.   The snow does'nt rise any higher than the horses' fetlocks. *[more than one horse]*

2.   For a bus driver, complaints, fare disputes, and endless questions are all part of a days work.

3.   Each day the menu features a different European countries' dish.

4.   We cleared four years accumulation of junk out of the attic; its amazing how much can pile up.

5.   Booties are placed on the sled dogs feet to protect them from sharp rocks and ice. *[more than one dog]*

6.   Sue and Ann went to a party for a friend of theirs'.

7.   Three teenage son's can devour about as much food as four full-grown field hands. The only difference is that they dont do half as much work.

8.   Ethiopians's meals were served on fermented bread.

9.   Luck is an important element in a rock musicians career.

10.   My sister-in-law's quilts are being shown at the Fendrick Gallery.

EXERCISE P6-1 Quotation marks If you have problems with this exercise, see pp. 214–20 in *A Canadian Writer's Reference*, Updated Second Edition.

Add or delete quotation marks as needed and make any other necessary changes in punctuation in the following sentences. If a sentence is correct, write "correct" after it. Answers to lettered sentences appear in the back of the booklet. Example:

> **Stephen Leacock once said, "I never realized that there was history too, close at hand, beside my very home."**

a. "Order in the court!" shouts the judge, banging her kitchen spoon on the kitchen table.

b. As Sir Ernest Rutherford said in 1902, I would like to take this opportunity to emphasize that the credit for the first definite proof of atomic transformation belongs to McGill University.

c. Andrew Marvell's most famous poem, To His Coy Mistress, is a tightly structured argument.

d. "Ladies and gentlemen," said the emcee, "I am happy to present our guest speaker."

e. Historians Segal and Stineback tell us that the English settlers considered these epidemics "the hand of God making room for His followers in the "New World"."

1. The dispatcher's voice cut through the still night air: "Car 41, robbery in progress, alley rear of 58th and King.

2. Dean Romero's letter warned me that "if I didn't drop the class I would receive a failing grade."

3. Kara looked hopelessly around the small locked room. "If only I were a flea," she thought, "I could get out of here."

4. My skiing instructor told us that "we would be ready for the intermediate slope in one week."

5. After the movie Vicki said, "The reviewer called this flick "trash of the first order." I guess you can't believe everything you read."

6. Gloria Steinem once twisted an old proverb like this, "A woman without a man is like a fish without a bicycle."

7. Joan was a self-proclaimed "rabid Blue Jays fan"; she went to every home game and even flew to Atlanta for the World Series.

8. As David Anable has written: "The time is approaching when we will be able to select the news we want to read from a pocket computer."

9. "Even when freshly washed and relieved of all obvious confections," says Fran Lebowitz, "children tend to be sticky."

10. Have you heard the Cowboy Junkies' rendition of "I'm So Lonesome I Could Cry?"

EXERCISE P7-1   The period, the question mark, and the exclamation point   If you have problems with this exercise, see pp. 220–23 in *A Canadian Writer's Reference*, Updated Second Edition.

Add appropriate end punctuation in the following paragraph.

Although I am generally rational, I am superstitious I never walk under ladders or put shoes on the table If I spill the salt, I go into frenzied calisthenics picking up the grains and tossing them over my left shoulder As a result of these curious activities, I've always wondered whether knowing the roots of superstitions would quell my irrational responses Superstition has it, for example, that one should never place a hat on the bed This superstition arises from a time when head lice were quite common and placing a guest's hat on the bed stood a good chance of spreading lice through the host's bed Doesn't this make good sense And doesn't it stand to reason that if I know that my guests don't have lice I shouldn't care where their hats go Of course it does It is fair to ask, then, whether I have changed my ways and place hats on beds Are you kidding I wouldn't put a hat on a bed if my life depended on it.

EXERCISE P7-2 Other punctuation marks If you have problems with this exercise, see pp. 223–27 in *A Canadian Writer's Reference*, Updated Second Edition.

Edit the following sentences to correct errors in punctuation, focusing especially on appropriate use of the dash, parentheses, brackets, ellipsis mark, and slash. If a sentence is correct, write "correct" after it. Answers to lettered sentences appear in the back of the booklet. Example:

> **Social insects/—bees, for example/—are able to communicate quite complicated messages to their fellows.**

a. We lived in New Brunswick (Fredericton, to be specific) during the early years of our marriage.

b. Every night—after her jazzercise class—Elizaveta bragged about how invigorated she felt, but she always looked exhausted.

c. John Humphrey said that "it turns out the achievement of 1948 [the Universal Declaration of Human Rights] was much greater than anybody would have dared to imagine at the time.

d. Every person there—from the youngest toddler to the oldest great-grandparent, was expected to sit through the three-hour sermon in respectful silence.

e. Every November 11 at our school assembly, we stand and recite "In Flanders fields the poppies grow—We shall not sleep, though poppies grow / in Flanders fields.

1. Of the three basic schools of detective fiction, the tea-and-crumpet, the hardboiled detective, and the police procedural, I find the quaint, civilized quality of the tea-and-crumpet school the most appealing.

2. In *Lifeboat*, Alfred Hitchcock appears (some say without his knowledge) in a newspaper advertisement for weight loss.

3. There are three points of etiquette in poker: 1. always allow someone to cut the cards, 2. don't forget to ante up, and 3. never stack your chips.

4. When he was informed that fewer than 20 percent of the panelists scheduled for the 1986 PEN conference were women, Norman Mailer gave this explanation: "There are more men who are deeply interested in intellectual matters than women . . . [If we put more women on the panel] all we'd be doing is lowering the level of discussion."

5. The old Valentine verse we used to chant said it all: "Roses are red, / Violets are blue, / Sugar is sweet, / And so are you."

EXERCISE P7-3 Punctuation review If you have problems with this exercise, see pp. 193–227 in *A Canadian Writer's Reference*, Updated Second Edition.

Punctuate the following letter.

72 Benson Ave

Toronto Ontario M1K 2J4

April 16 2000

Dear Rosalie

I have to tell you about the accident We were driving home at around 5 30 pm of course we'd be on Highway 401 at rush hour when a red Mustang smashed us in the rear Luckily we all had our seatbelts fastened Dr. Schabbles who was in the back seat and my husband Bob complained of whiplash but really we got off with hardly a scratch

The mother and daughter in the Mustang however weren't as fortunate They ended up with surgical collars and Ace bandages but their car certainly fared better than ours

The driver of the third car involved in the accident confused everyone Although her car was in the front of the line she kept saying I hit the tan car I hit the tan car We didn't understand until she told us that a fourth car had hit her in the rear and had pushed her ahead of all the rest Can you imagine how frustrated we were when we found out that this man the one who had started it all had left the scene of the accident You were the last car in line someone said No you were we answered The policeman had to reconstruct the disaster from the hopeless babble of eight witnesses

Its uncanny Out of 34800 cars on the highway on April 14 the police keep count you know our car had to be the one in front of that sporty red Mustang

Well I just wanted to send you a report I hope your days are less thrilling than mine

Yours

Marie

EXERCISE S1-1 Spelling If you have problems with this exercise, see pp. 231–35 in *A Canadian Writer's Reference*, Updated Second Edition.

Ask a friend or classmate to dictate the following paragraph to you. When you have transcribed it, check your version with this one. Note any words that you misspelled and practise writing them correctly.

The members of a faculty committee that recommends changes in course requirements invited several students to meet with them. In their invitation, the members emphasized that even though they would ask specific questions, they especially wanted the students to discuss their experience in various courses and to offer suggestions for changes. The students who were chosen represented a variety of academic interests, and the committee particularly selected students who were in their first year and in their last year. In his separate interview with the committee, John, who is graduating in May, questioned whether it was necessary to take so many courses that were apparently unrelated to his business major. He acknowledged that the requirement for some courses outside his major was legitimate; however, he believed that more thorough preparation for his specialty, international finance, would have been appropriate. John was worried because the job market had become so competitive, and he did not feel that he had benefited from some of the courses he had taken outside the business school. John apologized for being so negative, and he praised the committee for its willingness to listen to the opinions of students.

EXERCISE S1-2 Spelling If you have problems with this exercise, see pp. 231–35 in *A Canadian Writer's Reference*, Updated Second Edition.

The following paragraphs have been run through a spell checker on a computer. Proofread them carefully, editing the spelling and typographical errors that remain.

Later, John wrote a letter to the faculty committee, describing the kinds of classes that had had the greatest affect on him. John's letter impressed the committee, because he was able to site specific professors and specific teaching method. He started his letter very candidly: "Even though your professors, I must say that the best learning experiences I had did not involve the professor, accept as a resource or as a guide." John explained that he achieved more when he was actively involved in the class then when he sat and listened to the professor lecturing and asking questions.

John praised one professor in particular, an imminent psychologist and author. "When Professor Howell past control to the class," wrote John, "we took this as a complement. We had all assumed that being subjected to lengthy, boring lectures was a fundamental principal in higher education, but Professor Howell proved us wrong." In his letter, John went on to describe how the class was taught. Professor Howell asked each student to give reports, and she regularly had small groups discuss material or solve specific problems and report to the class. She participated in the class, to, but students had more access to her as she circulated though the room to answer questions or to challenge students to think in different ways. John closed his letter with further praise for Professor Howell and for teachers like her, saying, "Their what I'll remember most about my educational experiences in university."

EXERCISE S2-1   The hyphen   If you have problems with this exercise, see pp. 236–38 in *A Canadian Writer's Reference*, Updated Second Edition.

Edit the following sentences to correct errors in hyphenation. If a sentence is correct, write "correct" after it. Answers to lettered sentences appear in the back of the booklet. Example:

> **Zola's first readers were scandalized by his slice-of-life novels.**

a. Gold is the seventy-ninth element in the periodic table.

b. The quietly-purring cat cleaned first one paw and then the other before curling up under the stove.

c. The Moche were a pre-Columbian people who established a sophisticated culture in ancient Peru.

d. Your dog is well-known in our neighbourhood.

e. Dmitri did fifty push-ups in two minutes and then collapsed.

1. We knew we were driving too fast when our tires skidded over the rain slick surface.

2. The Black Death reduced the population of some medieval villages by two thirds.

3. The flight attendant asked us to fasten our seatbelts before takeoff.

4. One-quarter of the class signed up for the debate on Canadian involvement in NAFTA.

5. Joan had been brought up to be independent and self reliant.

EXERCISE S3-1 Capital letters If you have problems with this exercise, see pp. 238–42 in *A Canadian Writer's Reference*, Updated Second Edition.

Edit the following sentences to correct errors in capitalization. If a sentence is correct, write "correct" after it. Answers to lettered sentences appear in the back of the booklet. Example:

Bay of Fundy   Gaspé Peninsula

On our trip to the East we visited the b̶ay of f̶undy and the g̶aspé p̶eninsula.

a. Crown attorney Johnson was disgusted when the jurors turned in a verdict of not guilty after only one hour of deliberation.

b. My mother has begun to research the history of her acadian ancestors in New Brunswick.

c. W. C. Fields's epitaph reads, "On the whole, I'd rather be in Philadelphia."

d. Immigrants from europe are finding it more and more difficult to cross the Atlantic ocean into Canada.

e. I want to take Environmental Biology 103, one other Biology course, and one English course.

1. "O Liberty," cried madame Roland from the scaffold, "What crimes are committed in thy name!"

2. The grunion is an unremarkable fish except for one curious habit: it comes ashore to spawn.

3. Does your Aunt still sing in the local theatre productions whenever she's asked?

4. Historians have described Robert E. Lee as the aristocratic south personified.

5. My brother is a Doctor and my sister-in-law is an Attorney.

EXERCISE S4-1 Abbreviations If you have problems with this exercise, see pp. 242–45 in *A Canadian Writer's Reference*, Updated Second Edition.

Edit the following sentences to correct errors in abbreviations. If a sentence is correct, write "correct" after it. Answers to lettered sentences appear in the back of the booklet. Example:

Christmas   Friday.

This year ~~Xmas~~ will fall on a ~~Fri.~~

a. Audrey Hepburn was a powerful spokesperson for UNICEF for many years.

b. Denzil spent all night studying for his psych. exam.

c. "Mahatma" Gandhi has inspired many modern leaders, including Martin Luther King, Jr.

d. The first discovery of North America was definitely not in 1492 A.D.

e. Turning to p. 195, Marion realized that she had finally reached the end of ch. 22.

1. Social expectations change over time—e.g., in my mother's generation, women were expected to stay home and raise the children.

2. Three interns were selected to assist the chief surgeon, Dr. Enrique Derenzo, M.D., in the hospital's first heart-lung transplant.

3. Some historians think that the New Testament was completed by A.D. 100.

4. My soc. prof. spends most of his lecture time talking about political science.

5. Since its inception, the BBC has maintained a consistently high standard of radio and television broadcasting.

EXERCISE S5-1 Numbers If you have problems with this exercise, see pp. 245–46 in *A Canadian Writer's Reference*, Updated Second Edition.

Edit the following sentences to correct errors in the use of numbers. If a sentence is correct, write "correct" after it. Answers to lettered sentences appear in the back of the booklet. Example:

$3.06
By the end of the evening Ashanti had only ~~three dollars and six cents~~ left.

a. We have ordered 4 azaleas, 3 rhododendrons, and 2 mountain laurels for the back area of the garden.

b. Venezuelan independence from Spain was declared on July 5, 1811.

c. The score was tied at 5–5 when the momentum shifted and carried the Expos to a decisive 12–5 win.

d. We ordered three four-door sedans for company executives.

e. The Vietnam Veterans Memorial in Washington, D.C., had fifty-eight thousand one hundred thirty-two names inscribed on it when it was dedicated in 1982.

1. One of my favourite scenes in Shakespeare is the property division scene in Act I of *King Lear*.

2. The botany lecture will begin at precisely 3:30 P.M.

3. 90 of the firm's employees signed up for the insurance program.

4. After her 5th marriage ended in divorce, Melinda decided to give up her quest for the perfect husband.

5. With 6 students and 2 teachers, the class had a 3:1 student–teacher ratio.

EXERCISE S6-1   Italics (underlining)   If you have problems with this exercise, see pp. 246–48 in *A Canadian Writer's Reference*, Updated Second Edition.

Edit the following sentences to correct errors in the use of italics. If a sentence is correct, write "correct" after it. Answers to lettered sentences appear in the back of the booklet. Example:

> **<u>The Diviners</u> by Margaret Laurence was quite controversial when it was published twenty years ago.**

a. Howard Hughes commissioned the Spruce Goose, a beautifully built but thoroughly impractical wooden aircraft.

b. Pulaski was so *exhausted* he could barely lift his foot the fifteen centimetres to the elevator floor.

c. Even though it is almost always hot in Mexico in the summer, you can usually find a cool spot on one of the park benches in the town's *zócalo*.

d. Cinema audiences once gasped at hearing the word *damn* in *Gone With the Wind*.

e. "Dance of the Happy Shades" was an early novel by Alice Munro.

1. Bernard watched as Eileen stood transfixed in front of Vermeer's Head of a Young Girl.

2. The nursery walls were painted with scenes from her favourite bed-time stories.

3. I learned the Latin term ad infinitum from an old nursery rhyme about fleas: "Great fleas have little fleas upon their back to bite 'em. / Little fleas have lesser fleas and so on ad infinitum."

4. Redford and Newman in the movie "The Sting" were amateurs compared with the seventeen-year-old con artist who lives at our house.

5. I find it impossible to remember the second *l* in *llama*.

EXERCISE B1-1 Parts of speech: nouns If you have problems with this exercise, see p. 361 in *A Canadian Writer's Reference*, Updated Second Edition.

Underline the nouns (and noun/adjectives) in the following sentences. Answers to lettered sentences appear in the back of the booklet. Example:

> Idle <u>hands</u> are the <u>devil's</u> <u>workshop</u>.

a. Clothe an idea in words, and it loses its freedom of movement.   — *Egon Freidell*

b. Pride is at the bottom of all great mistakes.   — *John Ruskin*

c. The trouble with being in the rat race is that even if you win, you're still a rat.

                                                                             — *Lily Tomlin*

d. Perhaps the most striking thing about Canada is that it is not part of the United States.
                                                                           — *J. Bartlett Brebner*

e. Figures won't lie, but liars will figure.   — *Anonymous*

1. Conservatism is the worship of dead revolutions.   — *Clinton Rossiter*

2. The Canadian winter is a cold and excessive mistress.   — *Howard O'Hagan*

3. Problems are only opportunities in work clothes.   — *Henry Kaiser*

4. A woman must have money and a room of her own.   — *Virginia Woolf*

5. Prejudice is the child of ignorance.   — *William Hazlitt*

EXERCISE B1-2   Parts of speech: pronouns   If you have problems with this exercise, see pp. 361–63 in *A Canadian Writer's Reference*, Updated Second Edition.

Underline the pronouns (and pronoun/adjectives) in the following sentences. Answers to lettered sentences appear in the back of the booklet. Example:

Beware of persons <u>who</u> are praised by <u>everyone</u>.

a. Every society honours its live conformists and its dead troublemakers.

— *Mignon McLaughlin*

b. Watch the faces of those who bow low.   — *Polish proverb*

c. I have written some poetry that I myself don't understand.   — *Carl Sandburg*

d. This is the flag of the future, but it does not dishonour the past.   — *Lester B. Pearson*

e. I must govern the clock, not be governed by it.   — *Golda Meir*

1. A Canadian is somebody who knows how to make love in a canoe.   — *Pierre Berton*

2. Nothing is interesting if you are not interested.   — *Helen MacInness*

3. We will never have friends if we expect to find them without fault.   — *Thomas Fuller*

4. The gods help those who help themselves.   — *Aesop*

5. You never find yourself until you face the truth.   — *Pearl Bailey*

EXERCISE B1-3   Parts of speech: verbs   If you have problems with this exercise, see pp. 363–65 in *A Canadian Writer's Reference*, Updated Second Edition.

Underline the verbs in the following sentences, including helping verbs and particles. If a verb is part of a contraction (such as *is* in *isn't* or *would* in *I'd*), underline only the letters that represent the verb. Answers to lettered sentences appear in the back of the booklet. Example:

A full cup <u>must</u> <u>be</u> <u>carried</u> steadily.

a. Great persons have not commonly been great scholars.   — *Oliver Wendell Holmes, Sr.*

b. Without the spice of guilt, can sin be fully savoured?   — *Alexander Chase*

c. One arrow does not bring down two birds.   — *Turkish proverb*

d. If love is the answer, could you please rephrase the question?   — *Lily Tomlin*

e. Don't scald your tongue in other people's broth.   — *English proverb*

1. Do not needlessly endanger your lives until I give you the signal. — *Dwight D. Eisenhower*

2. The road to ruin is always kept in good repair.   — *Anonymous*

3. Love your neighbour, but don't pull down the hedge.   — *Swiss proverb*

4. I'd rather have roses on my table than diamonds around my neck.   — *Emma Goldman*

5. He is a fine friend. He stabs you in the front.   — *Leonard Louis Levinson*

EXERCISE B1-4   Parts of speech: adjectives and adverbs   If you have problems with this exercise, see pp. 365–66 in *A Canadian Writer's Reference*, Updated Second Edition.

Underline the adjectives and circle the adverbs in the following sentences. If a word is a pronoun in form but an adjective in function, treat it as an adjective. Also treat the articles *a*, *an*, and *the* as adjectives. Answers to lettered sentences appear in the back of the booklet. Example:

A wild goose never laid a tame egg.

a. General notions are generally wrong.   — *Lady Mary Wortley Montagu*

b. The American public is wonderfully tolerant.   — *Anonymous*

c. Gardening is not a rational act.   — *Margaret Atwood*

d. Hope is a very thin diet.   — *Thomas Shadwell*

e. Sleep faster. We need the pillows.   — *Yiddish proverb*

1. I'd rather be strongly wrong than weakly right.   — *Tallulah Bankhead*

2. Their civil discussions were not interesting, and their interesting discussions were not civil.
                                   — *Lisa Alther*

3. Money will buy a pretty good dog, but it will not buy the wag of its tail.   — *Josh Billings*

4. A little sincerity is a dangerous thing, and a great deal of it is absolutely fatal.

                                   — *Oscar Wilde*

5. An old quarrel can be easily revived.   — *Italian proverb*

EXERCISE B2-1   Parts of sentences: subjects   If you have problems with this exercise, see pp. 368–69 in *A Canadian Writer's Reference*, Updated Second Edition.

In the following sentences, underline the complete subject and write *ss* above the simple subject(s). If the subject is an understood *you*, insert it in parentheses. Answers to lettered sentences appear in the back of the booklet. Example:

<u>Fools and their money</u> are soon parted.

a. A spoiled child never loves its mother.   — *Sir Henry Taylor*

b. To some lawyers, all facts are created equal.   — *Felix Frankfurter*

c. Speak softly and carry a big stick.   — *Theodore Roosevelt*

d. There is nothing permanent except change.   — *Heraclitus*

e. The only difference between a rut and a grave is their dimensions.   — *Ellen Glasgow*

1. The secret of being a bore is to tell everything.   — *Voltaire*

2. Don't be humble. You're not that great.   — *Golda Meir*

3. In every country dogs bite.   — *English proverb*

4. The wind and the waves are always on the side of the ablest navigators.   — *Anonymous*

5. There are no signposts in the sea.   — *Vita Sackville-West*

EXERCISE B2-2 Parts of sentences: objects and complements If you have problems with this exercise, see pp. 370–72 in *A Canadian Writer's Reference*, Updated Second Edition.

Label the subject complements, direct objects, indirect objects, and object complements in the following sentences. If an object or complement consists of more than one word, bracket and label all of it. Answers to lettered sentences appear in the back of the booklet. Example:

$$\text{DO} \qquad \text{OC}$$
All work and no play make Jack a dull boy.

a. The best mind-altering drug is truth.   — *Lily Tomlin*

b. No one tests the depth of a river with both feet.   — *West African proverb*

c. All looks yellow to a jaundiced eye.   — *Alexander Pope*

d. Luck never made a man [or a woman] wise.   — *Seneca the Younger*

e. You show me a capitalist and I will show you a bloodsucker.   — *Malcolm X*

1. Accomplishments have no colour.   — *Leontyne Price*

2. Gardening is an exercise in optimism.   — *Marina Schinz*

3. The mob has many heads but no brains.   — *Thomas Fuller*

4. I never promised you a rose garden.   — *Hannah Green*

5. Moral indignation is jealousy with a halo.   — *H. G. Wells*

EXERCISE B3-1   Subordinate word groups: prepositional phrases   If you have problems with this exercise, see pp. 372–73 in *A Canadian Writer's Reference*, Updated Second Edition.

Underline the prepositional phrases in the following sentences. Be prepared to explain the function of each phrase. Answers to lettered sentences appear in the back of the booklet. Example:

> **You can stroke people <u>with words.</u>** (Adverbial phrase modifying <u>can stroke</u>)

a.   Laughter is a tranquilizer with no side effects.   — *Arnold Glasgow*

b.   Any mother could perform the job of several traffic controllers with ease.   — *Lisa Alther*

c.   She wears her morals like a loose garment.   — *Langston Hughes*

d.   You can tell the ideals of a nation by its advertising.   — *Norman Douglas*

e.   In prosperity, no altar smokes.   — *Italian proverb*

1.   We know that the road to freedom has always been stalked by death.   — *Angela Davis*

2.   A society of sheep produces a government of wolves.   — *Bertrand de Jouvenal*

3.   Some people feel with their heads and think with their hearts.   — *G. C. Lichtenberg*

4.   In love and war, all is fair.   — *Francis Edward Smedley*

5.   On their side, the workers had only the Constitution. The other side had bayonets.
                                                    — *Mother Jones*

EXERCISE B3-2 Subordinate word groups: verbal phrases If you have problems with this exercise, see pp. 373–74 in *A Canadian Writer's Reference*, Updated Second Edition.

Underline the verbal phrases in the following sentences. Be prepared to explain the function of each phrase. Answers to lettered sentences appear in the back of the booklet. Example:

Do you want <u>to be a writer</u>? Then write. (Infinitive phrase used as direct object of <u>Do want</u>)

a. The best substitute for experience is being sixteen. *— Raymond Duncan*

b. Fate tried to conceal him by naming him Smith. *— Oliver Wendell Holmes, Jr.*

c. Scandal is gossip made tedious by morality. *— Oscar Wilde*

d. Being a philosopher, I have a problem for every solution. *— Robert Zend*

e. For years I wanted to be older, and now I am. *— Margaret Atwood*

1. The thing generally raised on city land is taxes. *— C. D. Warner*

2. Do not use a hatchet to remove a fly from your friend's forehead. *— Chinese proverb*

3. He has the gall of a shoplifter returning an item for a refund. *— W. I. E. Gates*

4. I don't deserve any credit for turning the other cheek as my tongue is always in it. *— Flannery O'Connor*

5. Concealing a disease is no way to cure it. *— Ethiopian proverb*

EXERCISE B3-3 Subordinate word groups: subordinate clauses If you have problems with this exercise, see pp. 374–75 in *A Canadian Writer's Reference*, Updated Second Edition.

Underline the subordinate clauses in the following sentences. Be prepared to explain the function of each clause. Answers to lettered sentences appear in the back of the booklet. Example:

> **Dig a well <u>before you are thirsty</u>.**   (Adverb clause modifying <u>Dig</u>)

a. It is hard to fight an enemy who has outposts in your head. — *Sally Kempton*

b. An idea that is not dangerous is unworthy to be called an idea at all. — *Elbert Hubbard*

c. When I am an old woman, I shall wear purple. — *Jenny Joseph*

d. Dreams say what they mean, but they don't say it in daytime language. — *Gail Godwin*

e. A fraud is not perfect unless it is practised on clever persons. — *Arab proverb*

1. What history teaches us is that we have never learned anything from it.
    — *Georg Wilhelm Hegel*

2. When a dog is drowning, everyone offers him a drink. — *George Herbert*

3. Whoever named it necking was a poor judge of anatomy. — *Groucho Marx*

4. I never met a girl who matched up to Lois Lane. — *Joe Shuster*

5. He gave her a look that you could have poured on a waffle. — *Ring Lardner*

EXERCISE B4-1 Sentence types If you have problems with this exercise, see pp. 375–77 in *A Canadian Writer's Reference*, Updated Second Edition.

Identify the following sentences as simple, compound, complex, or compound-complex. Be prepared to identify the subordinate clauses and classify them according to their function: adjective, adverb, or noun. (See B3-e.) Answers to lettered sentences appear in the back of the booklet. Example:

The frog in the well knows nothing of the ocean. simple

a. When I scored that final goal, I finally realized what democracy was all about.
— *Paul Henderson*

b. My folks didn't come over on the Mayflower; they were there to meet the boat.
— *Will Rogers*

c. No pessimist ever discovered the secrets of the stars, or sailed to an uncharted land, or opened a new heaven to the human spirit. — *Helen Keller*

d. If you don't go to other people's funerals, they won't go to yours. — *Clarence Day*

e. Tell us your phobias, and we will tell you what you are afraid of. — *Robert Benchley*

1. Seek simplicity and distrust it. — *Alfred North Whitehead*

2. Those who write clearly have readers; those who write obscurely have commentators.
— *Albert Camus*

3. The children are always the chief victims of social chaos. — *Agnes Meyer*

4. The field of our dreams is flooded and frozen and has a net at either end. — *Joey Slinger*

5. When an elephant is in trouble, even a frog will kick him. — *Hindu proverb*

Answers to Lettered Exercises

EFFECTIVE SENTENCES

EXERCISE E1-1 Parallelism   *page 1*

Possible revisions:

a. The system has capabilities such as communicating with other computers, processing records, and performing mathematical functions.
b. The personnel officer told me that I would answer the phone, welcome visitors, distribute mail, and do some typing.
c. Nolan helped by cutting the grass, trimming shrubs, mulching flowerbeds, and raking leaves.
d. How ideal it seems to raise a family here in Cap de la Madeleine instead of in the air-polluted suburbs.
e. Michiko told the judge that she had been pulled out of a line of fast-moving traffic and that she had a perfect driving record.

EXERCISE E2-1 Needed words   *page 2*

Possible revisions:

a. Myra was both interested in and concerned about the contents of her father's will.
b. A few of the day-care services are similar to those of the public schools.
c. SETI (the Search for Extraterrestrial Intelligence) has excited and will continue to excite interest among space buffs.
d. Samantha got along better with the chimpanzees than with Albert. [*or* . . . than Albert did.]
e. We were glad to see that Jasper National Park was recovering from the devastating forest fire.

EXERCISE E3-1 Misplaced modifiers   *page 3*

Possible revisions:

a. He wanted to buy only three roses, not a dozen.
b. Within the next few years, orthodontists will be using as standard practice the technique Kurtz developed.
c. Celia received a flyer from a Japanese nun about a workshop on making a kimono.
d. Jurors are encouraged to sift through the evidence carefully and thoroughly.
e. Each province would set into motion a program of recycling all reusable products.

EXERCISE E3-2 Dangling modifiers   *page 4*

Possible revisions:

a. Reaching the heart, the surgeon performed a bypass on the severely blocked arteries.
b. When I was nestled in the cockpit, the pounding of the engine was muffled only slightly by my helmet.
c. While we dined at night, the lights along the Baja coastline created a romantic atmosphere perfect for our first anniversary.
d. While my sister was still a beginner at tennis, the coaches recruited her to train for the Olympics.
e. After Marcus Garvey returned to Jamaica, his "Back to Africa" movement slowly died.

EXERCISE E4-1 Shifts   *page 5*

Possible revisions:

a. The young man who burglarized our house was sentenced to probation for one year, a small price to pay for robbing us of our personal possessions as well as of our trust in other human beings.
b. After the count of three, Mikah and I placed the injured woman on the scoop stretcher. Then I took her vital signs.
c. Ministers often have a hard time because they have to please so many different people.
d. We drove for eight hours until we reached the Alberta Badlands. We could hardly believe the eeriness of the landscape at dusk.
e. The question is whether ferrets bred in captivity have the instinct to prey on prairie dogs or whether this is a learned skill.

EXERCISE E5-1 Mixed constructions   *page 6*

Possible revisions:

a. My instant reaction was anger and disappointment.
b. I brought a problem into the house that my mother wasn't sure how to handle.
c. It is through the misery of others that old Harvey has become rich.
d. A cloverleaf allows traffic on limited-access freeways to change direction.
e. Bowman established the format that future football card companies would emulate for years to come.

EXERCISE E6-2 Coordination and subordination *page 8*

Possible revisions:

a. My grandfather, who has dramatic mood swings, was diagnosed as manic-depressive.
b. The losing team was made up of superstars who acted as isolated individuals on the court.
c. Because Chantal had helped François through school, he decided to do the same for her.
d. The aides help the children with their weakest subjects, reading and math.
e. My first sky dive, from an altitude of 4200 metres, was the most frightening experience of my life.

EXERCISE E6-3 Faulty subordination   *page 9*

Possible revisions:

a. During a routine morning at the clinic, an infant in cardiac arrest arrived by ambulance.
b. My 1969 Camaro, an original SS396, is no longer street legal.
c. When I presented the idea of job sharing to my supervisors, to my surprise they were delighted with the idea.
d. Although outsiders have forced changes on them, some aboriginal groups try to preserve their ancestors' sacred customs.
e. Sophia's country kitchen, formerly a lean-to porch, overlooks a field where horses and cattle graze among old tombstones.

WORD CHOICE

EXERCISE W1-1 Usage   *page 11*

Possible revisions:

a. The number of horses a Blackfoot warrior had in his possession indicated the wealth of his family.

b. The cat just sat there watching his prey.
c. We will telephone you as soon as the tickets arrive.
d. Correct
e. Habib redesigned the boundary plantings to try to improve the garden's overall design.

EXERCISE W2-1   Wordy sentences   *page 12*

Possible revisions:

a. The drawing room in the west wing is said to be haunted.
b. Dr. Singh has seen problems like yours countless times.
c. Bloom's race for the premiership is futile.
d. New fares must be reported to our transportation offices in Montreal, Ottawa, and Toronto
e. In the heart of Beijing lies the Forbidden City, an imperial palace built during the Ming dynasty.

EXERCISE W3-1   Jargon and pretentious language*page 14*

Possible revisions:

a. It is a widely held myth that middle-aged people can't change.
b. Have you ever been accused of beating a dead horse?
c. In 1985 I bought a house in need of repair.
d. When Sal was laid off from his high-paying factory job, he learned what it was like to be poor.
e. Passengers should try to complete the customs declaration form before leaving the plane.

EXERCISE W3-3   Sexist language   *page 16*

Possible revisions:

a. Asha Purpura is the defence attorney appointed by the court. Al Jones has been assigned to work with her on the case.
b. A young graduate who is careful about investments can accumulate a significant sum in a relatively short period.
c. An elementary school teacher should understand the concept of nurturing if he or she intends to be a success.
d. Because Dr. Brown and Dr. Coombs were the senior professors in the department, they served as co-chairpersons of the promotion committee.
e. If we do not stop polluting our environment, we will perish.

EXERCISE W4-1   Active verbs   *page 17*

Possible revisions:

a. Her letter acknowledged the students' participation in the literacy program.
b. Ahmed, the producer, manages the entire operation.
c. Emphatic and active; no change.
d. Players were fighting on both sides of the rink.
e. Emphatic and active; no change.

EXERCISE W4-2   Misused words   *page 18*

Possible revisions:

a. Many of us are not persistent enough to make a change for the better.
b. It is sometimes difficult to hear in church because the acoustics are so terrible.
c. Tyrone has a presumptuous attitude.
d. When bp nichol died at age forty, he left a legacy of poems that will make him immortal.
e. This patient is kept in isolation to prevent her from catching our germs.

EXERCISE W4-3   Standard idioms   *page 19*

Possible revisions:

a. Queen Anne was so angry with Sarah Churchill that she refused to see her again.
b. Correct
c. Try to come up with the rough outline, and Marika will fill in the details.
d. For the frightened refugees, the dangerous trek across the mountains was preferable to life in a war zone.
e. The parade moved off the street and onto the beach.

EXERCISE W4-4   Clichés and mixed figures of speech   *page 20*

Possible revisions:

a. Pierette told Kyle that keeping secrets would be dangerous.
b. The prime minister thought that the scientists were using science as a means of furthering their political goals.
c. Ours was a long courtship; we waited ten years before finally deciding to marry.
d. We ironed out the wrinkles in our relationship.
e. Sasha told us that he wasn't willing to take the chance.

GRAMMATICAL SENTENCES

EXERCISE G1-1   Subject–verb agreement   *page 21*

a. Subject: friendship and support; verb: have; b. Subject: rings; verb: are; c. Subject: Each; verb: was; d. Subject: source; verb: is; e. Subject: signs or remnants; verb: were.

EXERCISE G1-2   Subject–verb agreement   *page 22*

a. High concentrations of carbon monoxide result in headaches, dizziness, unconsciousness, and even death.
b. Correct
c. Correct
d. Crystal chandeliers, polished floors, and a new oil painting have transformed Sandra's apartment.
e. Either Gertrude or Alice takes the dog out for its nightly walk.

EXERCISE G2-1   Irregular verbs   *page 24*

a. Noticing that my roommate was shivering and looking pale, I rang for the nurse.
b. When I get the urge to exercise, I lie down until it passes.
c. Grandmother had driven our new jeep to the cottage on Georgian Bay, so we were left with the station wagon.
d. I just heard on the news that Michael Smith has broken the world record for the long jump.
e. Correct

EXERCISE G2-2   *-s* and *-ed* verb forms and omitted verbs   *page 25*

a. Correct
b. The museum visitors were not supposed to touch the exhibits.
c. Our church has all the latest technology, even a closed-circuit television.
d. We often don't know whether he is angry or just joking.
e. Staggered working hours have reduced traffic jams and saved motorists many litres of gas.

EXERCISE G2-3   Verb tense and mood   *page 26*

a.   Correct
b.   Watson and Crick discovered the mechanism that controls inheritance in all life: the workings of the DNA molecule.
c.   In 1941 Hitler decided to kill the Jews. But Himmler and his SS were three years ahead of him; they had had mass murder in mind since 1938.
d.   Toni could be an excellent student if she weren't so distracted by problems at home.
e.   Correct

EXERCISE G3-1   Pronoun–antecedent agreement   *page 28*

Possible revisions:

a.   I can be standing in front of a photocopier, with parts scattered around my feet, and someone will ask me for permission to make a copy.
b.   Correct
c.   The instructor has asked everyone to bring his or her own tools to carpentry class.
d.   An eighteenth-century architect was also a classical scholar who was often at the forefront of archeological research.
e.   On the first day of class, Mr. Bhatti asked each of us why we wanted to stop smoking.

EXERCISE G3-3   Pronoun reference   *page 30*

Possible revisions:

a.   The detective photographed the body after removing the blood-stained shawl.
b.   In Professor Jamal's class, students are lucky to earn a C.
c.   Please be patient with the elderly residents who have difficulty moving through the cafeteria line.
d.   The settlers lived difficult lives; they had to clear acres of trees and cope with an extreme climate.
e.   All students can secure parking permits from the campus police office, which is open from 8 A.M. until 8 P.M.

EXERCISE G3-4   Pronoun case: personal pronouns   *page 31*

a.   My Ethiopian neighbour was puzzled by the dedications of us joggers.
b.   Correct
c.   Sue's husband is ten years older than she.
d.   Everyone laughed whenever Sandra described how her brother and she had seen the Loch Ness monster and fed it sandwiches.
e.   Correct

EXERCISE G3-5   Pronoun case: *who* and *whom*   *page 32*

a.   In his first production of *Hamlet*, whom did Laurence Olivier replace?
b.   Correct
c.   Correct
d.   Some group leaders cannot handle the pressure; they give whoever makes the most noise most of their attention.
e.   One of the women whom Lanvis hired became the most successful lawyer in the agency.

EXERCISE G4-1   Adjectives and adverbs   *page 34*

a.   When Tina began breathing normally, we could relax.
b.   All of us on the team felt bad about our performance.
c.   Tim's friends cheered and clapped very loudly when he made it to the bottom of the beginners' slope.
d.   Correct
e.   Last Christmas was the most wonderful day of my life.

EXERCISE G5-1   Sentence fragments   *page 35*

Possible revisions:

a.   As I stood in front of the microwave, I recalled my grandmother bending over her old black stove and remembered what she taught me: that any food can have soul if you love the people you are cooking for.
b.   It has been said that there are only three indigenous American art forms: jazz, musical comedy, and soap opera.
c.   Correct
d.   We need to stop believing myths about drinking—that strong black coffee will sober you up, for example, or that a cold shower will straighten you out.
e.   As we walked up the path, we came upon the gun batteries, large grey concrete structures covered with ivy and weeds.

EXERCISE G6-1   Comma splices and fused sentences   *page 38*

Possible revisions:

a.   The city had one public swimming pool that stayed packed with children all summer long.
b.   The building is being renovated, so at times we have no heat, water, or electricity.
c.   Why should we pay taxes to support public transportation? We prefer to save energy dollars by carpooling.
d.   We all make mistakes; no one is perfect.
e.   In Garvey's time the caste system in the West Indies was simple: the lighter the skin tone, the higher the status.

EXERCISE G6-2   Comma splices and fused sentences   *page 40*

Possible revisions:

a.   Because the trail up Mount Grossmore was declared impassable, we decided to return to our hotel a day early.
b.   Correct
c.   The instructor never talked to the class; she just assigned make-work and sat at her desk reading the newspaper.
d.   Researchers studying the fertility of Canada geese X-rayed all the female geese to see how many eggs they had.
e.   The suburbs seemed cold; they lacked the warmth and excitement of our Italian neighbourhood.

ESL TROUBLE SPOTS

EXERCISE T1-2   Articles   *page 45*

a.   Some of the best wine in the world comes from the Rhine River valley in southwestern Germany.
b.   Courage is an admirable characteristic.
c.   When I was at the park yesterday I saw a dog playing with a ball. I picked up the ball and threw it, and the dog chased after it.
d.   She got advice from her counsellor, but the advice was not as helpful as she had hoped.
e.   Beauty is a difficult concept to define.

EXERCISE T2-1   Helping verbs and main verbs   *page 46*

a.   We will make this a better country.
b.   There is nothing in the world that TV has not touched on.
c.   Did you understand my question?
d.   A hard wind was blowing while we were climbing the mountain.
e.   The child's innocent world has been taken away from him.

EXERCISE T2-3   Verbs in conditional sentences   *page 48*

Possible revisions:

a. He would have won the election if he had gone to the northern regions to campaign.
b. If Martin Luther King, Jr., were alive today, he would be appalled by the violence in the inner cities of the United States.
c. Whenever my uncle comes to visit, he brings me an expensive present.
d. We will lose our largest client unless we update our computer system.
e. If Verena wins a fellowship, she will go to graduate school.

EXERCISE T2-4   Verbs in conditional sentences   *page 49*

a. had worn or had been wearing; b. go; c. will earn; d. were; e. would improve

EXERCISE T2-5   Verbs followed by gerunds or infinitives   *page 50*

Possible revisions:

a. I enjoy riding my motorcycle.
b. Will you help Samantha study for the test?
c. The team hopes to work hard and win the championship.
d. Jules and his brothers miss surfing during the winter.
e. The babysitter let Roger stay up until midnight.

EXERCISE T2-6   Verbs followed by gerunds or infinitives   *page 51*

a. seeing, thinking; b. to pay, going; c. to write, to reply; d. living, getting; e. to be, knowing

EXERCISE T3-1   Omissions and repetitions   *page 52*

a. The roses they brought home cost three dollars each.
b. There are two grocery stores on Elm Street.
c. The prime minister is the most popular leader in my country.
d. Pavel hasn't heard from the cousin he wrote to last month.
e. The king, who had served since the age of sixteen, was an old man when he died.

EXERCISE T3-2   Order of cumulative adjectives   *page 53*

a. an attractive young Vietnamese woman
b. a dedicated Catholic priest
c. her old blue wool sweater
d. Joe's delicious Scandinavian bread
e. many beautiful antique bird cages

EXERCISE T3-3   Order and placement of adjectives and adverbs   *page 54*

a. We have two large grey cats; one of them has a small patch of white fur around his right eye.
b. The two men, who were young defence lawyers, wore long dark robes.
c. Most mornings he reluctantly ate his breakfast, and sometimes he refused to eat anything at all.
d. Correct
e. When I was a child, my friends and I built a wooden tree house in an enormous old oak tree.

EXERCISE T3-4   Present versus past participles   *page 55*

a. Having to listen to everyone's complaints was irritating.
b. The noise in the hall was distracting to me.

c. Correct
d. The violence in recent movies is often disgusting.
e. Correct

EXERCISE T3-5   Present versus past participles   *page 56*

a. interested; b. annoying; c. satisfied; d. exhausted; e. encouraging

EXERCISE T3-6   Prepositions showing time and place   *page 57*

Possible revisions:

a. We spent seven days in June at the beach, and it rained every day.
b. Correct
c. Usually she met with her patients in the afternoon, but on that day she stayed at home to take care of her son.
d. The clock is hanging on the wall in the dining room.
e. In Germany it is difficult for foreigners to become citizens even if they've lived in the country for a long time.

EXERCISE T3-7   Prepositions showing time and place   *page 58*

a. On, at; b. at, in, on; c. in, at, in; d. on, on; e. at, in

PUNCTUATION

EXERCISE P1-1   The comma: independent clauses, introductory elements   *page 59*

a. Correct
b. The man at the next table complained loudly, and the waiter stomped off in disgust.
c. Instead of eating half a cake or two dozen cookies, I now grab a banana or an orange.
d. Nursing is physically and mentally demanding, yet the pay is low.
e. Uncle Sven's dulcimers disappeared as soon as he put them up for sale, but he always kept one for himself.

EXERCISE P1-2   The comma: series, coordinate adjectives   *page 60*

a. She wore a black silk cape, a rhinestone collar, satin gloves, and high-tops.
b. There is no need to prune, weed, fertilize, or repot your air fern.
c. City Café is noted for its spicy vegetarian dishes and its friendly, efficient service.
d. Trevor walked through the room with casual, elegant grace.
e. Correct

EXERCISE P1-3   The comma: nonrestrictive elements   *page 61*

a. B. B. King and Lucille, his customized black Gibson, have electrified audiences all over the world.
b. My backpack, which is designed to last a lifetime, is wearing out.
c. Correct
d. Shakespeare's tragedy *King Lear* was given a splendid performance by the actor Laurence Olivier.
e. Correct

EXERCISE P1-4   Major uses of the comma   *page 62*

a. The whisky stills, which were run mostly by farmers and fishermen, were about thirty kilometres from the nearest town.

b. At the sound of a starting pistol, the horses surged forward toward the first obstacle, a sharp incline one metre high.
c. Each morning the seventy-year-old woman cleans the barn, shovels manure, and spreads clean hay around the milking stalls.
d. The students of Highpoint are required to wear dull green polyester pleated skirts.
e. Beauty is in the eye of the beholder, but glamour is for anyone who can afford it.

EXERCISE P1-5   All uses of the comma   *page 63*

a. April 13, 1995, is the final deadline for all applications.
b. The coach having bawled us out thoroughly, we left the locker room with his last, harsh words ringing in our ears.
c. Good technique does not guarantee, however, that the power you develop will be sufficient for Kyok Pa competition.
d. We all piled into Sadiq's car, which we affectionately referred to as the Blue Goose.
e. Please make the check payable to David Kerr, D.D.S, not David Kerr, M.D.

EXERCISE P2-1   Unnecessary commas   *page 64*

a. We'd rather spend our money on blue-chip stocks than speculate on pork bellies.
b. Being prepared for the worst is one way to escape disappointment.
c. When he heard the groans, he opened the door and ran out.
d. My father said that he would move to Nova Scotia if I would agree to transfer to Dalhousie.
e. I quickly accepted the fact that I was literally in third-class quarters.

EXERCISE P3-1   The semicolon and the comma   *page 65*

a. While there's snow on the roof, it doesn't mean the fire has gone out in the furnace.
b. No amount of experimentation can ever prove me right; a single experiment can prove me wrong.
c. Don't talk about yourself; it will be done when you leave.
d. The only sensible ends of literature are first, the pleasurable toil of writing; second, the gratification of one's family and friends; and lastly, the solid cash.
e. When men talk about defence, they always claim to be protecting women and children, but they never ask the women and children what they think.

EXERCISE P3-2   The semicolon and the comma   *page 66*

a. Many people believe that ferrets are vicious little rodents; in fact, ferrets are affectionate animals that tend to bite only out of fear.
b. Canada has been called a country with no identity, although the Canadian devotion to defining their identity is legendary.
c. The first requirement is honesty; everything else follows.
d. I am not fond of opera; I must admit, however, that I was greatly moved by *Les Misérables*.
e. Correct

EXERCISE P4-1   The colon, the semicolon, and the comma   *page 67*

a. The second and most memorable week of outdoor camp consisted of five stages; orientation, long treks, rock climbing, white-water rafting, and return to civilization.
b. Among the cancelled classes were calculus, physics, advanced biology, and English 101.
c. Correct
d. For example, Stephen Leacock once said that "the essence of humour is human kindliness."
e. Correct

EXERCISE P5-1   The apostrophe   *page 68*

a. In a democracy anyone's vote counts as much as mine.
b. Correct
c. The puppy's favourite activity was chasing its tail.
d. After we bought J.J. the latest style pants and shirts, he decided that last year's faded, ragged jeans were perfect for all occasions.
e. A crocodile's life span is about thirteen years.

EXERCISE P6-1   Quotation marks   *page 69*

a. Correct
b. As Sir Ernest Rutherford said in 1902, "I would like to take this opportunity to emphasize that the credit for the first definite proof of atomic transformation belongs to McGill University."
c. Andrew Marvell's most famous poem, "To His Coy Mistress," is a tightly structured argument.
d. Correct
e. Historians Segal and Stinebeck tell us that the English settlers considered these epidemics "the hand of God making room for His followers in the 'New World.'"

EXERCISE P7-2   Other punctuation marks   *page 71*

a. We lived in Fredericton, New Brunswick, during the early years of our marriage.
b. Every night after her jazzercise class, Elizaveta bragged about how invigorated she felt, but she always looked exhausted.
c. Correct
d. Every person there—from the youngest toddler to the oldest great-grandparent—was expected to sit through the three-hour sermon in respectful silence.
e. Every November 11 at our school assembly, we stand and recite "In Flanders fields the poppies grow.... We shall not sleep though poppies grown/in Flanders fields."

SPELLING AND MECHANICS

EXERCISE S2-1   The hyphen   *page 75*

a. Correct
b. The quietly purring cat cleaned first one paw and then the other before curling up under the stove.
c. The Moche were a pre-Columbian people who established a sophisticated culture in ancient Peru.
d. Your dog is well known in our neighbourhood.
e. Correct

EXERCISE S3-1   Capital letters   *page 76*

a. Crown Attorney Johnson was disgusted when the jurors turned in a verdict of not guilty after only one hour of deliberation.
b. My mother has begun to research the history of her Acadian ancestors in New Brunswick.
c. Correct
d. Immigrants from Europe are finding it more and more difficult to cross the Atlantic Ocean into Canada.
e. I want to take Environmental Biology 103, one other biology course, and one English course.

EXERCISE S4-1   Abbreviations   *page 77*

a. Correct
b. Denzil spent all night studying for his psychology exam.
c. Correct
d. The first discovery of North America was definitely not in A.D. 1492.
e. Turning to page 195, Marion realized that she had finally reached the end of chapter 22.

EXERCISE S5-1 Numbers *page 78*

a. We have ordered four azaleas, three rhododendrons, and two mountain laurels for the back area of the garden.
b. Correct
c. Correct
d. We ordered three 4-door sedans for company executives.
e. The Vietnam Veterans Memorial in Washington, D.C., had 58,132 names inscribed on it when it was dedicated in 1982.

EXERCISE S6-1 Italics (underlining) *page 79*

a. Howard Hughes commissioned the *Spruce Goose*, a beautifully built but thoroughly impractical wooden aircraft.
b. Pulaski was so exhausted he could barely lift his foot the fifteen centimetres to the elevator floor.
c. Even though it is almost always hot in Mexico in the summer, you can usually find a cool spot on one of the park benches in the town's *zócalo*.
d. Correct
e. *Dance of the Happy Shades* was an early novel by Alice Munro.

BASIC GRAMMAR

EXERCISE B1-1 Parts of speech: nouns *page 80*

a. idea, words, freedom, movement; b. Pride, bottom, mistakes; c. trouble, rat (noun/adjective), race, rat; d. thing, Canada, part, United States; e. Figures, liars

EXERCISE B1-2 Parts of speech: pronouns *page 81*

a. Every (pronoun/adjective), its (pronoun/adjective), its (pronoun/adjective); b. those, who; c. I, some (pronoun/adjective), that, I, myself; d. this, it; e. I, it

EXERCISE B1-3 Parts of speech: verbs *page 82*

a. have been; b. can be savoured; c. does bring down; d. is, could rephrase; e. Do scald

EXERCISE B1-4 Parts of speech: adjectives and adverbs *page 83*

a. Adjectives: General, wrong; adverb: generally; b. Adjectives: The (article), American, tolerant; adverb: wonderfully; c. Adjectives: a (article), rational; adverb: not; d. Adjectives: a (article), thin; adverb: very; e. Adjective: the (article); adverb: faster

EXERCISE B2-1 Parts of sentences: subjects *page 84*

a. Complete subject: A spoiled child; simple subject: child; b. Complete subject: all facts; simple subject: facts; c. Complete subject: (You); d. Complete subject: nothing except change; simple subject: nothing; e. Complete subject: The only difference between a rut and a grave; simple subject: difference

EXERCISE B2-2 Parts of sentences: objects and complements *page 85*

a. Subject complement: truth; b. Direct object: the depth of a river; c. Subject complement: yellow; d. Direct object: a man [or a woman]; object complement: wise; e. Indirect objects: me, you; direct objects: a capitalist, a bloodsucker

EXERCISE B3-1 Subordinate word groups: prepositional phrases *page 86*

a. with no side effects (adjective phrase modifying *tranquilizer*); b. of several air traffic controllers (adjective phrase modifying *job*), with ease (adverbial phrase modifying *could perform*); c. like a loose garment (adverbial phrase modifying *wears*); d. of a nation (adjective phrase modifying *ideals*), by its advertising (adverbial phrase modifying *can tell*); e. In prosperity (adverbial phrase modifying *smokes*)

EXERCISE B3-2 Subordinate word groups: verbal phrases *page 87*

a. being sixteen (gerund phrase used as subject complement); b. to conceal him (infinitive phrase used as direct object of *tried*), naming him Smith (gerund phrase used as object of the preposition *by*); c. made tedious by morality (participial phrase modifying *gossip*); d. Being a philosopher (participial phrase modifying *I*); e. to be older (infinitive phrase used as direct object of *wanted*)

EXERCISE B3-3 Subordinate word groups: subordinate clauses *page 88*

a. who has outposts in your head (adjective clause modifying *enemy*); b. that is not dangerous (adjective clause modifying *idea*); c. When I am an old woman (adverb clause modifying *shall wear*); d. what they mean (noun clause used as the direct object of *say*); e. unless it is practised on clever persons (adverb clause modifying *is*)

EXERCISE B4-1 Sentence types *page 89*

a. complex, When I scored that final goal (adverb clause); b. compound; c. simple; d. complex; If you don't go to other people's funerals (adverb clause); e. compound-complex; what you are afraid of (noun clause)